EQUIPPING PREACHERS
PASTORS & CHURCHMEN

Equipping Preachers Pastors & Churchmen

Selected Articles by
The Faculty of
Greenville Presbyterian
Theological Seminary

Presbyterian Press | Taylors, SC

PRESBYTERIAN PRESS

P.O. Box 690, Taylors, SC 29687, USA

864.322.2717 | gpts.edu

ISBN

Print: 978 1 931639 16 3

EPUB: 978 1 931639 17 0

Typeset, Cover Design, and Book Layout Completed at
Greenville Presbyterian Theological Seminary

Printed in the U.S.A. by
Versa Press, Inc.,
East Peoria, IL

CONTENTS

FOREWARD

During the winter and spring of 1985-1986, two seminary students approached Dr. Morton H. Smith about the need for a theological seminary that fully met "The Uniform Curriculum" adopted by the Presbyterian Church in America (PCA). They were joined by Pastor Paul Settle and Ruling Elder J. Ligon Duncan, Jr. of Second Presbyterian Church in Greenville, SC. On February 26, 1986, Mr. and Mrs. Duncan hosted a group including those named above and the Duncans' sons, Ligon, John, and Melton, in their home to discuss the possibility of moving forward with such a project. They agreed: the need for a seminary was present, and Greenville, SC was an ideal location.

Soon thereafter, the Session of Second Presbyterian Church formed a steering committee consisting of Pastor Settle, John C. Neville, Jr., Dr. Smith, the Elder Duncan, and C. Stuart Patterson. In the fall of 1987, Greenville Presbyterian Theological Seminary began equipping preachers, pastors, and churchmen for Christ's Kingdom, and the school has faithfully continued in this work ever since.

The seminary has experienced a number of significant changes over the past 30 years: three buildings, twenty-seven graduating classes, over 200 students, and many faithful professors, staff workers, and trustees who have served the seminary and its students at one time or another. Throughout, the faculty have remained committed to giving men the equipment needed to preach God's Word, pastor God's people, and serve God's church faithfully, carefully, and lovingly. this volume contains a small sampling of the kind of instruction Greenville Seminary students receive from our faculty.

We have collected[1] these articles in order to provide ministers and seminary students with a resource for their work as preachers, pastors, and churchmen. By no means is this collection of articles exhaustive. For example, there are no pieces dealing specifically with preaching, prayer, or sacraments, though the authors clearly present a vision for serving the church with the ordinary means of grace instituted by her Lord.

This collection does capture some of the emphases of our instruction. *Dr. Pipa* outlines the biblical basis and approach of the seminary in the first article, and the biblical understanding of gender roles in public worship in the last article. *Drs. Dyer, Morales, and Hamilton* bring to life the picture of a "Greenville Education" by presenting different facets of the faculty's approach to equipping men for the ministry. In a previously unpublished essay, *Dr. Shaw* explores the Problem of Evil from the book of Job. *Dr. McGoldrick* echoes John Calvin's call for a biblical understanding of vocation - as relevant to the churchmember as it is to the ordained churchman. *Dr. Curto* expresses the evangelistic mission of the church at home and abroad. *Drs. McGraw and Willborn* teach us how to serve as faithful churchmen in the courts of the church. We have also adapted and republished two works from *Drs. Smith and Knight* that systematically explain the commitment entailed by confessional subscription and the role of the Diaconate in the church.

Thanks are due to the faculty for taking such an active interest in this collection, and for graciously responding to my emails, phone calls, and in-person office visits. Thanks are also due to Mr. Garry Moes, who began the editorial work for this project before undergoing a massive heart surgery and long-distance relocation to California. Finally, thanks are due to my wife, Jocelyn, for sacrificing a number of evenings together as I combed through the copy and prepared the typeset for this book.

Zachary Groff, Editor

---

[1] Sources include academic journals, essay collections, denominational magazines, conferences, and even one General Assembly.

SEMINARY EDUCATION
by Joseph A. Pipa, Jr.

The nature of training men for ministry in Reformed churches is important because we take it for granted and, in the minds of many, the future of traditional, campus-based schools is up for grabs.

There is one other reason why this topic is important. We live in a time of knowledge overload, a time when many people in their fields are highly skilled and educated, a time of many more advanced degrees above the baccalaureate level such as MBAs, Masters, and PhDs. We come out of a tradition in which our ministers were normally the best educated of anybody in the culture, but that situation is far behind us.

I am involved in theological education at the seminary level because I believe that to a large degree the future of the Reformed seminary is the future of the Reformed church. If we are to see a blessing from God in the Reformed church, there are certain things that we ought to be doing in our seminaries, and so the future of the Reformed seminary is important.

The Bible clearly establishes the importance of ministerial training. For some examples look at 1 Timothy 4:11-16 and 2 Timothy 2:1,2,15.

We need to begin with the biblical and historical background for ministerial training. Why do we use seminaries? Is there a biblical basis for doing so? How did the whole idea of seminaries develop? Look up *Seminary* in the encyclopedia and you will probably learn that the seminary is a place where Roman Catholic priests are trained for the priesthood. So how in the world did seminaries develop in the

Protestant tradition and why do we use them?

Let's begin to answer our questions with an overview of the history of the training of ministers. When did this training begin? Apparently theological training schools were begun under Samuel. We find the first mention of the group or the company of the prophets in I Samuel 10:5,10 (see also 1 Samuel 19:19,20). 1 Kings 20:35; 2 Kings 2:3,5,15; 4:1,38; 5:22; 6:1 refer to the men involved as "son of the prophets." Under Samuel, the prophetic office developed in Israel. Men studied in these schools and prepared to serve as prophets. Normally, the prophets came from these schools.

The prophetic schools began in the days of Samuel and continued through the divided kingdom. These schools of prophets would have been similar to our theological schools. The men probably would have studied the law of God, since part of the prophetic office was to teach the law and interpret it in the context of the covenant and theocratic life of their day. So they would have been trained in the Scriptures and the interpretation of the Scriptures. Their training would have included history and historical writing, since they were the historians of the Old Covenant church (2 Chron. 12:15; 20:34 cf. 19:2). The training evidently included musical and poetical training, as they made use of musical instruments and songs in their ministry. They also employed elaborate literary structure, suggesting poetical training.

Now it is interesting to note that when a prophet preached or wrote he enjoyed the special work of the Holy Spirit. The prophets wrote many books of the Old Testament. In addition to the books bearing their names, they wrote the history books of Samuel, Kings and Chronicles. Since they had the Holy Spirit, why did they need to go to school? God used prepared men, men who studied for their task. We conclude, therefore, that the "school of the prophets" was basically an Old Covenant seminary.

In the New Testament we continue to find an emphasis on training. Christ chose the twelve that they might be with him (Mark 3:14). Paul himself spent three years in the desert in preparation (Gal.

1:17,18); Paul taught his young assistants and commanded Timothy to do the same (2 Tim. 2:1,2).

Note as well that within the "schools of the prophets" mentoring and discipleship played a very important role in the development of these men. God used mentoring relationships throughout biblical history to train men for ministry. Just consider Moses and Joshua; Elijah and Elisha; Christ and the twelve; Paul and his young men who traveled with him.

The concept of mentoring shows why those studying in the school of the prophets are called the "sons of the prophets." The prophets-in-training were in a father-son relationship with their teachers. Such relationships are essential to spiritual and ministerial formation and should be practiced in the church: pastors with elders, elders with other men in the church, women with other women in the church, parents with our children. One of our particular goals at Greenville Seminary is to keep a low student-faculty ratio so that we will never lose mentoring relationships between faculty and students. We recognize that we cannot accomplish our goals only in the classroom. Mentoring relationships must be developed and sustained.

Early on, the post-apostolic church manifested a commitment to ministerial training. The most famous early school was in Alexandria where Clement of Alexandria began the Catechetical School. Initially the purpose of the school was to train new converts. Eventually they began to train men for the ministry, and the Catechetical School of Alexandria became a theological center. Unfortunately, it was a theological center with a deviant foundation that caused a great deal of damage because of its allegorical approach of Scriptures and compromise with Greek philosophy. That school, to a great degree, shaped the direction of the church in the Middle Ages. Again we are reminded of the importance of theological education and the danger the seminary can be to the church. You must keep in mind that most error in a denomination comes from the place where she gets her ministers. All of our seminaries and educational institutions must be accountable to healthy churches; otherwise, they will eventually subvert the church.

Hardly a day passes that I do not think about the fact that no Christian institution of learning has ever remained faithful to God. This fact is sobering. Why is this the case? A number of reasons may be offered, but the two most important are seeking academic acclaim and failing to teach from an experimental point of view with love for God so that we do not turn our subject matter into abstractions. We must worship as we study, teach, and learn. Pray for us that we will be faithful, humble, and worshiping teachers.

In the Middle Ages, the educational level of the priests was abysmal, but the monasteries kept learning alive. The monks were, for the most part, better educated than the priests were. The monastic school tradition developed in Jerome's Monastery School in Palestine and Cassiodorus' Monastery School in Italy. Charlemagne and later Alfred the Great sponsored education reforms. Eventually schools developed around some of the great Cathedrals. In the twelfth century, the monastic schools and the cathedral schools coalesced into universities. The European universities gave rise to the development of scholasticism and laid the foundation for the revival of learning called the Renaissance. But it was really the Reformation that captured the universities and used them to prepare men for the ministry. Almost to a man, the Reformers were university men and they all placed a great emphasis on education.

With the Reformation came a whole system of Protestant universities following the pattern of Wittenberg. Initially the University of Wittenberg was the most significant powerhouse of the Reformation as men came from all over Europe to study with Luther and Melanchthon. In Geneva, one of Calvin's lifelong goals was to establish the Academy. Finally, in 1559, five years before he died, he was able to see the Academy established. Its primary purpose was to train men for the ministry.

The Reformers emphasized Greek and Hebrew in their teaching. The commitment to study the Scriptures in the languages of the Scripture was essential to the Reformation. The commitment to studying the Bible in the original languages is illustrated in Zwingli's method in Zurich. When he began his ministry he entered the pulpit with his

Hebrew and Greek Bible and began to expound the Scriptures. Today many ministers and seminaries disdain the possibility of a minister finishing seminary really knowing Greek and Hebrew. Yet, it was the knowledge of Greek and Hebrew that, in great part, the Spirit used to give birth to the Reformation. Let me give a very simple illustration: when Jerome translated the Latin Vulgate, he translated the word μετανοεο (*metanoeo*), which means "repentance" with a Latin idiom that meant "do penance". And thus for centuries the church based its doctrine of penance on this faulty translation.

Only as men began to read the New Testament in Greek did they properly understand the biblical concept was *repentance* and not *penance*. We are almost as bad off today when faulty English translations go unchallenged and Bible study notes are full of error. The Westminster Confession of Faith (1.8) insists that "in all controversies of religion, the Church is finally to appeal unto them (original languages of the Bible)." The Reformers understood this and so they instructed their students in the languages as well as in Biblical and Systematic Theology.

The Reformation also brought about a shift in the instruction of Homiletics (the study of preaching). Up to the time of the Reformation, Homiletics had been taught as a subset of classical rhetoric and Aristotelian logic. This approach destroyed preaching. With the Reformation, men began to understand the importance of preaching and that it should be taught as distinct from rhetoric and logic (not to say that these subjects are unimportant). The Reformers insisted that Homiletics be taught as a separate subject, according to its biblically defined purposes and scriptural principles. On the Continent, a man named Hyperius wrote a Homiletics textbook that revolutionized preaching. In England, William Perkins wrote a book to instruct English preachers in how to preach.

As you understand history, you realize that there is nothing new under the Sun. Today we find ourselves with the pre-Reformation problem of teaching preaching as a subset, not of rhetoric, but of communication theory. Today in many seminaries, communication theory has usurped the role of classical homiletics. Though rhetoric and communication theory are helpful, we must teach homiletics as a distinct discipline.

For the most part, the training of ministers was carried on through the universities through the eighteenth century. The Puritans made great use of Cambridge and Oxford to train young ministers, but they also used the concept of mentoring. Prospective ministers went to live with seasoned pastors to develop their pastoral skills.

When the Puritans came to New England, they brought with them this commitment to theological education. John Harvard gave the funds to establish Harvard so that the colony would have a well-trained ministry. Fifty-two percent of the seventeenth-century Harvard graduates became ministers. When Harvard began to slip, Yale was formed. When Yale began to slip, Princeton developed. In fact, all but one of the Ivy League schools started as Christian schools. Dartmouth was started to train missionaries to send them overseas. William and Mary began for the propagation of the Gospel. This was the commitment that our Reformed forefathers - Congregational, Anglican, and Presbyterian - brought to our country. American Presbyterianism carried on this tradition in the nineteenth century.

Having laid the biblical and historical foundation for ministerial training, I want to focus on the particular method that developed in America. We inherited the university system of training men for the ministry, but other systems had developed as well. In England, the Nonconformists developed divinity halls to train ministers. Meanwhile in Scotland, churches utilized the parsonage system, in which a young man would attach himself to a mature minister to study and prepare.

In America, in addition to the University system, some began to implement the parsonage approach to ministerial education. Sometimes it would be less formally organized; a young man would go and live with a minister to learn informally from him through reading and joining in pastoral labors. Oftentimes though, the arrangement was more formal, and a young man would attach himself to a pastor to read divinity. There would be a set curriculum. The candidate would read and discuss with his mentor and thus prepare for the ministry.

The parsonage system, though, was inefficient for a country that was experiencing rapid growth. A more efficient system was needed to produce a sufficient number of trained ministers to keep up with the growth of our country. So out of the parsonage system the Academy developed. In the Academy (the most famous being the Log College), a group of students would live with and study under a minister. But the need remained to train a larger number of men; so in the late eighteenth-century, the forerunner of seminaries developed. Three schools began: the Dutch Reformed developed one in New York; a group of Associated Presbyterians developed one in Geneva, Pennsylvania; and the Associate Reformed Church developed one in New York. Each of these schools had one faculty member, a small library, and very few students.

A number of people saw the need for a well-endowed school that had more than one faculty member and a good library. In 1808, the Congregationalists in New England developed Andover Theological Seminary in Connecticut. Before they started, they had amassed a large library and endowment. They began with three full-time faculty members. This school was the first seminary. Three years later, in 1811, the Presbyterians started Princeton Theological Seminary. In 1812, the Reformed Church in America started New Brunswick Theological Seminary. Remarkably, in a five-year span three seminaries were begun in the Northeast and in fifty years sixty seminaries had been started in America. These schools laid the foundation for the Protestant seminary system of education in America, which system is now the dominant way men prepare for the ministry. Westminster Theological Seminary basically was formed on the plan of Old Princeton. When Dr. Morton Smith and others started Reformed Theological Seminary and later Greenville Presbyterian Theological Seminary, he used the plan of Old Princeton. In a sense, Greenville Seminary is a grandchild of Old Princeton.

Now the exciting thing today is that we can combine the best of seminary tradition with mentoring. Not only do faculty members mentor students, but also our students must work in local churches. Moreover, with the advent of distance education, we are seeing the rise of parsonage and presbytery-centered training.

We live in a day with amazing resources. We need to pray that God will raise up godly men and that our seminaries will labor to provide the churches with an academic, confessional, and practical program for ministerial training. Why should we settle for less?

Joseph A. Pipa, Jr. (PhD, Westminster Theological Seminary) is President of Greenville Presbyterian Theological Seminary, and Professor of Historical & Systematic Theology. This chapter was adapted from his "Seminary Education," in The Confessional Presbyterian, *2007, 223-230. Used by permission.*

PASTORAL USE OF BIBLICAL LANGUAGES

by Sidney Dyer

INTRODUCTION

Those who teach Biblical languages are obligated not only provide excellent instruction, they are also to motivate their students by convincing them that their call to the ministry requires proficiency in the languages. The rigors of the pastorate will make it difficult for graduates to maintain their competency in the languages. Thus, they must be convicted that their calling requires them to work with the original text and that their efforts will provide them with an accurate and fruitful understanding of the text. Instructors must also motivate their students by repeatedly showing them the benefits of their studies. Thus, this chapter provides incentives for knowing Greek and Hebrew.

Institutions that train men for the ministry must provide their students with thorough instruction in Greek and Hebrew. Failure to attain proficiency is one of the major obstacles to the pastoral use of the languages. A minister who repeatedly struggles to exegete his sermon texts and finds little benefit from his efforts will soon dispense with working in the original languages. Thus, this chapter offers suggestions for language instruction.

Motivation

Kendall H. Easley expresses a common concern among those who teach biblical languages when he laments that his labors in the classroom were apparently wasted because most of his former students stopped using Greek.[1] Students need more than just information. They obviously need motivation.

The Minister's Call and the Use of Original Languages

Language instructors must repeatedly remind their students that a minister is called by God to preach His Word, not translations. Translations are not the Word of God, but the work of fallible men and are the Word of God only to the extent that they agree with the original. There is no such thing as a 100 percent accurate translation. The numerous translations now on the market differ significantly among themselves. How is a minister to determine which one presents the most accurate rendering without proficiency in Biblical languages? A. T. Robertson points out that "there is much that cannot be translated. It is not possible to reproduce the delicate turns of thought, the nuances of the language, in translation. The freshness of the strawberry cannot be preserved in any extract."[2] It is imperative that schools training men to be preachers provide courses that will enable their students to achieve competency in Greek and Hebrew. A minister, who is ignorant of the original languages, is not capable of determining to what extent the passages he preaches from agree with the original. Thus, in order to be a reliable expositor of the Scriptures, a minister must know the original languages.

Some would argue that Greek is important for a preacher to know, but not Hebrew. In the preface to his grammar, C. L. Seow complains that most schools training ministers have made Hebrew an

---

1 He writes: "Much of my professional ministry as a college and seminary teacher has involved teaching Greek. After teaching for several years, I discovered that most of my former students- overwhelmed with the time demands of ministry-had let their Greek "rust out." What they had worked aggressively and diligently in the classroom to master was laid aside. Apparently, my labors in the Greek classroom had been wasted on these students." *User-Friendly Greek: A Common Sense Approach to the Greek New Testament* (Nashville: Broadman and Holman, 1994), vii.
2 *The Minister and His Greek New Testament* (Grand Rapids: Baker Book House, 1977), 17.

elective or scaled it down to teaching a mere "working knowledge."[3] Many institutions have undoubtedly removed Hebrew from their required curriculum or scaled it down because of the opinion that the New Testament is more important than the Old. The authors of the New Testament, however, did not share this attitude. Martin Luther correctly observed that "it is the intention of all the apostles and evangelists in the New Testament to direct and drive us to the Old Testament which they call the Holy Scriptures proper."[4] Paul teaches in 2 Timothy 3:16 that *all* Scripture is profitable for doctrine, reproof, correction, and instruction in righteousness. Thus, the Old Testament is as important for the sanctification of believers as the New Testament. The Old Testament is over three times larger than the New Testament. This means that a minister who knows only Hebrew would be able to study more Scripture in the original than one who knows only Greek. This, of course, does not mean we should teach Hebrew rather than Greek. Robert Chisholm points out that many students "sense there is a gulf between language study and sermon preparation."[5] He suggests that the Hebrew professor may have thought the homiletics professor would have bridged the gulf and that the homiletics professor may not have learned how to use the language himself and already has plenty to do teaching the organization, content, and delivery of sermons.[6]

If students do not recognize the practical usefulness of the languages for sermon preparation, they will fail to continue their endeavors in the languages after they graduate. Walter Kaiser, Jr. is undoubtedly correct that it is not the homiletical department, but the Biblical

3   He states: "Biblical Hebrew is an endangered field in Christian theology. Whereas it once was required that all ministerial candidates have competence in the language, most institutions involved in the training of ministers now offer Hebrew only as an elective, a luxury for the curious and a burden for the unfortunate. A few bodies hang on to the requirements of a "working knowledge" – something tantamount to the ability to impress one's congregation with a few Hebrew words or, at best, the ability to represent the opinion of others" *A Grammar for Biblical Hebrew* (Nashville: Abingdon Press, 1987), vii.

4   *Sermons of Martin Luther*, ed. John N. Lenker, (Grand Rapids, Mich.: Baker Book House, 1989), I, 31.

5   *From Exegesis to Exposition* (Grand Rapids: Baker, 1998), 9.

6   Ibid. He states: "But usually no one has built this bridge for the student. Perhaps the Hebrew professor thought the homiletics professor would build the bridge, but the homiletics professor may have never learned how to use the language himself, and, besides, he has enough to do teaching the would-be preacher how to organize material, gesture properly, choose good illustrations, and eliminate nasty communication flaws. The seminary has failed him by not forcing its professors to work more closely together and/or by not allowing room in the curriculum for professors to build the exegetical bridge linking language study with preaching."

exegesis department that has the primary responsibility to show the student how to move from the text to the sermon.[7] Students must especially be instructed not be preach nothing more than a technically commentary on the text.

Language instructors will find that the example of John Brown of Haddington, born in 1722, to be useful to motive their students. He was one of the great preachers and theologians of Scotland in his day. At the age of 16 he stepped into a bookstore and asked for a Greek New Testament. Some local professors had also entered the store and one of them told John that if he could read it, he would pay for it. John took the New Testament, and to the astonishment of all in the store, he read a passage. He walked out of the store with his gift. Young John Brown had taught himself Greek by comparing a borrowed copy of the Greek New Testament to English and Latin translations. He created his own Greek lexicon and by comparing Latin word endings with Greek word endings he made his own Greek grammar. Later he learned Hebrew. Young John Brown puts every seminary student and minister to shame who does not have a similar zeal for God s Word.

THE SIGNIFICANCE OF WORDS

Language instructors should seek to teach students the importance of knowing the precise meaning of words and the significance of a word's meaning in specific contexts. For example, in the KJV, Paul commands us in Galatians 6:2 to "bear one another s burdens." But in verse 5 he writes, "For every man shall bear his own burden." In the English this seems like a contradiction. In these texts, however, different words are both translated "burden." The word in verse 2 refers to an excessive load and the one in verse 5 refers to a normal load. Paul's teaching is that each man is to bear a normal load, but if the circumstances of his life become overwhelming, we are to help him. Daniel B. Wallace includes a humorous story in his grammar involving the use of the word "all." A country preacher, who did not know Greek, misunderstood the Lord's words of instruction in Matthew 26:27 in the KJV. It reads, "Drink ye all of it." The preacher

---

7 *Toward an Exegetical Theology* (Grand Rapids: Baker, 1981), 21-22.

understood the instruction to mean that all the wine had to be consumed. The church had a tradition of filling a pitcher with wine for each weekly communion service. The congregation had dwindled, but the preacher felt duty bound to drink all that remained in the pitcher after the people left. Thus, each Sunday he was getting drunk after the service.[8] In the Greek, the word "all" is in the nominative case. Jesus did not command the disciples to drink all the wine, but that they all were to partake of it.

In Genesis 18:19 the LORD says concerning Abraham, "For I know him, that he will command his children, and his household after him, and they shall keep the way of the LORD, to do justice and judgment." The word translated "that" is not a conjunction introducing what the LORD knows, but one that expresses purpose or result. Thus, what the LORD actually said was, "For I know him, in order that he may command his children."

GRAMMATICAL ANALYSIS

Language instructors must strive to demonstrate to their students the value of grammatical analysis and to correct some of the common grammatical errors that have spread. Perhaps the most common grammatical error in Greek is the misunderstanding of the third person imperative. The construction is normally translated with *let.* This, however, gives the impression that those addressed are passively to allow what is commanded to occur. Supplying the word *must* brings out the correct meaning. Thus, a better translation of Colossians 3:16 would be, "the word of Christ must dwell in you richly instead of "let the word of Christ dwell in you richly."[9]

The aorist tense is normally not significant. Dana and Mantey, however, explain that "the aorist may be used for stating a present reality with the certitude of a past event."[10] In John 13:31, Jesus says, "Now the Son of Man is glorified and God is glorified in Him." The

8 *Greek Grammar Beyond the Basics* (Grand Rapids: Zondervan, 1996), 372.

9 For the grammars that gives the correct understanding see, James A. Brooks and Carlton L. Winberry, *Syntax of New Testament Greek* (Lanham MD: University Press of America, 1979), 129, and Wallace, p. 486.

10 *A Manual Grammar of the Greek New Testament* (New York: The MacMillan Co., 1955), 198.

verb translated "is glorified" is in the aorist tense to express Jesus' certainty that He is being glorified. He spoke those words to the disciples immediately after Judas left to betray Him. Leon Morris states, "Now that the betrayal is under way the glorification of the Son has begun."[11] It had begun and would certainly reach its fullness.

Psalm 12:7 shows the importance of knowing Hebrew grammar in order to correctly interpret a text. The closest antecedent to the word "them" in the statement "You shall keep them, O LORD" is "words" in verse 6. The masculine plural pronominal suffix on the verb "shall keep," however, shows that the "them" points back to the "poor" and "needy" in verse 5, which are also masculine. The terms translated "words" in verse 6 are both feminine. Thus, the verse teaches that it is the poor and needy that the LORD will keep, rather than His words.

EMPHASIS

Emphasis is especially important to stress with students because the Greek and Hebrew had various ways of expressing it that are difficult to translate into English. Thus, a preacher who only works from his English Bible may miss a significant element in the text. In both Greek and Hebrew, when the author deviates from normal word order he is expressing emphasis. This is particularly true of words that stand at the beginning of a clause. In Galatians 2:20 the emphasis is on Christ. The Greek reads "with Christ I am crucified." In Genesis 9:13 we read, "I do set my bow in the cloud;" but in the Hebrew "my bow" stands emphatically at the beginning of the verse.

In John 18:33, Pilate asks Jesus, "Are You the king of the Jews?" The question contains the nominative pronoun "you" for emphasis. Richard Young explains that the emphatic use of a nominative pronoun can convey surprise.[12] This is surely the case in John 18:33. Pilate undoubtedly expected to see a wild-eyed, raging insurrectionist. The One who stood before was the complete opposite.

---

11 *The Gospel According to John* (Grand Rapids: Eerdmans, 1971), 630.
12 *Intermediate New Testament Greek* (Nashville, Broadman and Holman, 1994), 72.

The Use of Hebrew Grammar to Interpret the New Testament

Students need to know that Hebrew is useful for properly understanding some portions of the New Testament. In Hebrews 4:3, the Greek literally reads, "if they shall enter into my rest." But it is translated, "they shall not enter My rest." Why? Because it is a quotation from the Old Testament and the clause represents the Hebrew oath formula, which is characterized by a missing apodosis expressing self-imprecation. Thus, the phrase does indeed mean they would certainly not enter God's rest, but the certainty is expressed more emphatically with the oath formula. The same construction appears in Mark 8:12.

Insufficiency of Merely Using Helps

Over forty years ago, Greek professor James L. Boyer argued that a mere working knowledge of the original languages is inadequate.[13] Today the focus of so many seminaries is practical theology, and training in the languages is reduced to teaching students to use helps. One, however, cannot be sure that the language helps he uses are always accurate. We tend to think that computer programs are always reliable. That simply is not the case. Though the tools available to us are generally excellent, we must be informed enough ourselves to be able to double-check them.

Methodology

There are three primary factors that frequently are mentioned for why graduates fail to keep up with their Biblical languages: a lack of motivation, the time demands on the ministry, and the failure to gain adequate competence in the languages before graduation. These are interrelated problems. A graduate may be motivated to keep up with the language, but the demands on his time do not allow it. The reason he does not have enough time may be because it takes him too

---

13   He wrote: "The best preparation for proper Biblical exegesis, particularly in matters of semantics, the meaning of words, including both lexical and grammatical study, is the widest possible experience with and constant practice in the use of the original languages. One dare not look up a word in the analytical lexicon, discover it is a verb in the aorist tense, turn to the aorist section of Dana and Mantey, then say, 'The original Greek says so and so.'" "Semantics in Biblical Interpretation," *Grace Journal* 3 (1962), 33.

long to get anything significant from the original text. The reason he struggles to get anything out of the text may be because he was not sufficiently trained in the languages. Thus, methodology is actually another factor in motivating students to keep up with their languages and even to progress beyond what they learned during their formal education.

NEED FOR BASICS IN ENGLISH GRAMMAR

The state of the American educational system is so poor that many graduate from high school and college without knowing the basics of English grammar. Instructors are more likely to succeed when they assume that their students have little or no understanding of English grammar and who instruct their students in the basics. J. W. Wenham actually begins his Greek grammar with summary of English grammar.[14] The English grammarian H. Sweet correctly affirms that "the study of English grammar is the best possible preparation for the study of foreign languages."[15]

DISCOURSE ANALYSIS

God not only inspired every word of Scripture, He also inspired the manner in which those words have been set down in their relation to each other. This includes not only the words of a sentence, but also the relationship of one sentence to another and one paragraph to another. The first step of discourse analysis is to prepare a display of the coordination and subordination of paragraphs, sentences, clauses, and phrases. The next step is to label the relationship between these elements. A sentence may be a main proposition. Another may support a main proposition through reiteration, explanation, argumentation, application, etc. The purpose is to study a passage as a whole, as a single unit of communication.

Ideally, a discourse analysis will result in a sermon or lesson outline that is based on the structure and flow of the text. *Sometimes* the

14   *The Elements of New Testament Greek* (New York: Cambridge University Press, 1965), 1-16.
15   "Pedagogic Grammars" in *Grammar and Second Language Teaching: A Book of Readings,* William Rutherford and Michael S. Smith, eds. (New York: Newbury House Publishers, 1988), 125.

sequence of a text will not lend itself to a preaching outline that follows the sequence. Regardless, the structural analysis is a useful backdrop for the message as the preacher or teacher moves through his points. Discourse analysis is properly understood to be the crown of the exegetical process.

CONCLUSION

Those who are training ministers must endeavor to provide them with competence in biblical languages and with motivation to continue in their study once they are in the ministry. One primary means of motivating them is to persuade them that their call demands competency in Greek and Hebrew. Another is to repeatedly present them with exegetically significant examples from both the Hebrew Bible and the Greek New Testament. We should always seek to improve our teaching methods so that graduates leave our institutions with confidence that they can properly handle the Word of God from the original and accurately expound it from the pulpit. We dare not fail in this endeavor, not only because it would be a detriment to our graduates and their ministries, but also to Church by impeding its progress. Daniel Wallace said it well:

> If there is to be another Reformation--and I think one is sorely needed--knowledge of and hunger for the biblical languages will again form a vital component in its formation. Rather than a reaction to the excesses of Roman Catholicism, the next Reformation will be a reaction, in part, to the anti-intellectualism that has infested and corrupted evangelical theology, evangelical ministry, and evangelical life.[16]

May the Lord use this generation of evangelical language instructors and ministers to help effect another Reformation in our day.

Sidney Dyer (PhD, Bob Jones University) is Professor of Greek and New Testament at Greenville Presbyterian Theological Seminary. This chapter was adapted from his "Encouraging the Pastoral Use of Biblical Languages: Motivation and Methodology," a paper presented at the 2003 Southeastern Regional Meeting of the Evangelical Theological Society. Used by permission.

16 Editorial note at the beginning of Burer's article "The Place of Greek and Hebrew in a Minister's Education."

THE GLORY OF GOD'S HOUSE

by L. Michael Morales

What is the Sabbath?
...The Sabbath is an ascent to the summit.
- Abraham Joshua Heschel

The instructions for making the lampstand of the tabernacle s holy place describe it as a stylized almond tree, hammered out of pure gold, and having a central shaft with three branches on either sideall made "according to the pattern" which was shown to Moses on the mountain of God (Exod. 25:31-40). YHWH gives Aaron the high priest of Israel the particular duty of tending the lampstand in the following manner:

> And YHWH spoke to Moses saying: "Speak to Aaron, and say to him, When you set up the lamps, the seven lamps shall give light in front of the lampstand." And Aaron did so; he set up the lamps to face toward the front of the lampstand, as YHWH commanded Moses. Now this workmanship of the lampstand was hammered gold; from its base to its flowers it was hammered work. According to the pattern which YHWH had shown Moses, so he made the lampstand. (Num. 8:1-4):[1]

In his commentary on this passage, Gordon J. Wenham notes that the text is insistent on one point in particular, namely, on Aaron's duty to direct the menorah s seven lamps forward, ensuring they give light in front of the lampstand. Why such emphasis upon this curious duty of ensuring the lamps beam their light in front of the lampstand? He

---

[1] All translations are the author's own, unless otherwise stated.

explains that the meaning of this action becomes apparent when the design of the holy place is taken into account (emphasis added):

> If the light beamed forwards it would have fallen on the table of shewbread, where twelve loaves of bread, symbolizing the twelve tribes of Israel, were heaped up (Lev. 24:5-9). Light and fire represent the life-giving presence and blessing of God (e.g. Exod. 13:21-22). Thus Aaron had to arrange the lamps so that their light always illuminated the shewbread. *This arrangement portrayed visually God's intention that his people should live continually in his presence and enjoy the blessing mediated by his priests.*[2]

Wenham further remarks that this priestly duty symbolizes what the Levitical blessing in Num. 6:23-27 affirms verbally:[3]

> YHWH bless you and keep you;
> YHWH make his face shine upon you
>   and be gracious to you;
> YHWH lift up his face upon you
>   and give you peace.

So shall they put my Name upon the sons of Israel, and I myself will bless them.

This blessing, which in the Hebrew utilizes a three-fold use of the divine Name plus twelve remaining words, is itself not free of symbolic import. Here two brief observations are in order. First, the divine blessing, in both Num. 6 and 8, is portrayed as God's shining his light upon his people, which is further explained as putting "his Name" upon them (6:27) - a significant gloss to which we will return later on in this book. Secondly, the significance of the lampstand should be understood together with that of the bread of the presence, forming one symbolic picture, just as the light of God's countenance in the Levitical blessing of Num. 6 is cast upon his people. Indeed, the forward-facing arrangement of the lamps are an integral part of the instructions for manufacturing the lampstand (Exod. 25:37), inti-

---

2 *Numbers: An Introduction and Commentary* (Leicester: Inter-Varsity Press; Downers Grove: InterVarsity Press, 2008), 106-107.
3 Ibid., 107.

mately woven into its meaning, not to mention that these instructions follow immediately upon the directions to "set the bread of the Presence before me always" (v. 30). Aaron's instructions require, then, the readers awareness of the breads position before the lampstand in the holy place: according to Exod. 26:35 (cf. 40:24), the golden table with the twelve loaves of bread, was placed on the north side of the holy place, and the golden, seven-branched lampstand was set directly across from it on the south side (the tabernacle itself facing eastward).

In summary, the light of the lampstand represents the life-giving Presence of God, his blessed glory, while the twelve loaves represent the twelve tribes of Israel. Aaron's role of regularly arranging the lamps so that they shine upon the loaves summarizes the role and function of the priesthood to mediate God's blessings to his people. One might say, in short, that these references in Numbers summarize the role of the cultus for Israel's relationship with God, as it relates to the goal of the covenant.[4] Numbers 6:23-27 and 8:1-4 present the blessing of God upon the people of God, mediated by the priesthood of God.

The arrangement of the holy place of the tabernacle, therefore, portrayed the ideal of Israel basking in the light of the divine Presence in the house of God, abiding in the fires of his glory. As we will come to understand in the following chapters, this cultic symbolism depicted the Sabbath day in particular, as Israel entered the renewing Presence of YHWH *through the Levitical way* he had opened for them - a foretaste of life at the consummation of history. Indeed, this glimpse into the glory of the house of God may be appreciated more fully when we recall that the paneled walls of the holy place were overlaid with gold, a feature which, together with the golden lampstand and golden table, would have caused the light of the seven lamps to be reflected in a wondrous manner. And so this symbolic picture of Israel abiding in the blessed Sabbath day Presence of YHWH is one that portrays life in the house of God, a prospect foretasted in Israels Sabbath day worship.

---

4   As A.S. Kapelrud expresses it, "That ladder [of Jacob's dream, connecting heaven and earth] symbolizes the role of the cult in old Israel." from "The Role of the Cult in Old Israel" in *The Bible in Modern Scholarship: Papers Read at the 100th Meeting of the Society of Biblical Literature, December 28-30, 1964,* J.P. Hyatt, ed. (Nashville: Abingdon, 1965), 56.

Life with God in the house of God - this was the original goal of the creation of the cosmos (which, as we will come to see, may be thought of as a house), and which then became the goal of redemption, the new creation. The prophets offer glimpses of this reality in their descriptions of God's final redemption of his people; when, after he has purged and cleansed them and made them utterly holy, he dwells with them on his holy mountain.

> Then YHWH will create over the whole place of
>   Zion's mountain, and over her assemblies,
> a cloud by day and smoke, and the shining
>   of a flaming fire by night -
> for over all the glory there will be a canopy.
>
> (Isa. 4:5)

> "For I will be to her [Jerusalem]" - utterance of YHWH -
>   "a wall of fire surrounding her,
> and I will be the glory in her midst."
>
> (Zech. 2:5)

In the closing pages of John's Apocalypse, we are given a final glimpse of holy Jerusalem "having the glory of God," afire with such radiance from YHWH God that there will be neither night nor need of the sun (Rev. 21:10-11, 23; 22:5) as God's people dwell in the light of his glory. This consummation of the messianic kingdom of God is presented to us by John as the historical fulfillment of the divine intention, as expressed in the covenant formula:

> And I heard a loud voice from heaven saying, Look! The tabernacle of God is with humanity and he will dwell with them, and they shall be his people and God himself will be with them and be their God.
>
> (Rev. 21:3)

As the innermost aim of the covenant, dwelling with God in the house of God, for fullness of life in abundant joy and fellowship, is the great promise held out before God's people, and the ardent desire expressed in Israel's liturgy:

I will dwell in the house of YHWH forever.

(Ps. 23:6)

Those whom YHWH brings into his house receive divine hospitality. Much like a magnanimous ancient near eastern host, God spreads a table for his guests, anointing their heads with oil and pouring wine liberally into their cups (Ps. 23:5). Indeed, YHWHs house is described as the source of all life and abundance:

> They are abundantly satisfied with the
>   fatness of your house,
> And you give them drink from the
>   river of your pleasures ['dn].
> For with you is the spring of life;
> In your light we see light.

(Ps. 36:8-9)

Note the allusion to Eden's river of life, with the word "pleasures" being merely the plural form of "Eden." Dwelling in the house of God is, more deeply, a hope enflamed with the longing to behold YHWH himself - for he is the fountain of life:

> You will make known to me the path of life;
> There is fullness of joy in your Presence;
> And pleasures at your right hand forevermore.

(Ps. 16:9-11)

> O YHWH, I love the habitation of your house
> And the place where your glory dwells.

(Ps. 26:8)

The same yearning, to dwell with YHWH for a life suffused by the beatific vision, is expressed as the "one thing" the psalmist asks for in Psalm 27:4:

> One thing I have asked of YHWH - that will I seek:
> That I may dwell in the house of YHWH
>   all the days of my life,

To behold the beauty of YHWH,
And to contemplate in his temple.

But just here the question comes: how can this be possible? How is it that God's own abode may become the end of his peoples journey? How can becoming a member of the household of God be a real hope for creatures made from dust? Considering that only the high priest had been allowed entrance into the holy of holies within the tabernacle and later temple, how is it songs could be sung about dwelling in YHWHs house "forever" and "all the days of my life"? In many ways, this is the fundamental question of Israel's cult - and, indeed, of life itself:

> O YHWH, who may abide in your tabernacle?
> Who may dwell on your holy mountain?
>
> (Ps. 15:1)

> Who may ascend the mountain of YHWH?
> Or who may stand in his holy place?
>
> (Ps. 24:3)

This question of ascending God's mountain to his house was likely recited by pilgrims upon approaching the temple on Mount Zion during the annual pilgrimage festivals, and is referred to as a gate (or entrance) liturgy. As we will see in the chapters ahead, the gate liturgy runs as an undercurrent throughout the narratives of the Pentateuch, and is found at the heart of its central book, Leviticus. Such a point comes as no surprise when we consider that the Pentateuch itself is a thoroughly Levitical work, a priestly torah, whose traditional author, Moses, was a thorough-going Levite (Exod. 2:1-2; 6:14-27) - its dominating concern, as well as that of the rest of the Bible, is the way in which humanity may come to dwell in the house of God. Under the Mosaic covenant, that way opened up by YHWH was through the tabernacle and later temple, its priesthood and rituals - that is, through the Levitical cult. The advent of Christ would open up a new and living way into the house of God - indeed, that was the goal of his taking our humanity upon himself, of his suffering, of his resurrection and ascension.

This biblical theology of Leviticus, then, is a book about the theme of dwelling with God in the house of God, and how that reality is finally made possible. As Israel's deepest hope, to dwell in YHWHs house upon his holy mountain was not merely a liturgical question but a historical quest. A gravely confounding quest, to be sure, for who may "dwell with the devouring fire?" (Isa. 33:14). And yet Israel's destiny, nevertheless, is to become just such a wonder, akin to the burning bush, to be "burning with fire, but not consumed," alight with the glory of the Presence of God (Exod. 3:2-3). In Exodus 15, having just seen the deliverance of YHWH through the sea, Moses leads Israel in song, perhaps the most ancient in scripture. The theological heart and structural center of the song, v. 11, is the adoration of God, asking:

Who is like you, O YHWH, among the gods?
Who is like you, glorious in holiness,
fearful in praises,
doing wonders?

Again, we are confronted with "the deepest and innermost nature of the God of the Old Testament,"[5] his absolute holiness. From the heavens, the angels declare, "holy, holy, holy, is YHWH of hosts" (Isa. 6:3), that is, YHWH is like "no other." This heavenly indicative is matched by an earthly interrogative. From the earth, Israel, having experienced his salvation, cries up, "Who is like you, O YHWH?" The question itself is the highest acclamation of praise. And yet, even in the depths of such fearful marvel, the song moves on with undaunted hope to a nearly unimaginable promise - namely, that God's people have been delivered precisely for the purpose of abiding with this One to whom none can be compared (vv. 13, 17):

You in your loving-kindness will lead forth the people
you have redeemed;
You will guide them by your strength to your holy
habitation...
You will bring them in and plant them in the mountain
of your inheritance,

5   Ernst Sellin, *Theologie des Alten Testaments* (Leipzig: Quelle & Meyer, 1936), 19.

In the place, O YHWH, you have made for your
   own dwelling,
The sanctuary, O Lord, which your hands have
   established.

                                    (Exod. 15:13, 17)

The emphatic threefold "you will" of these verses is the source of
Israel's life and hope for dwelling in Gods house. YHWH, out of an
eternal love, purposes to make a way - and, is anything too difficult
for God? Anchored thus to YHWH's own will, his peoples longing
will not be in vain.

The Heidelberg Catechism, question and answer six, teaches that humanity was created to truly know and love God and to live with him
in eternal happiness, all to his praise and glory. Similarly, the Westminster Confession of Faith Shorter Catechism, question and answer
one, states that humanity's chief end is to glorify God and enjoy him
forever. These historic confessions capture precisely the biblical theology of the Bible. Entering the house of God to dwell with God, be-
holding, glorifying, and enjoying him eternally, I suggest, is *the* story
of the Bible, the plot which makes sense of the various acts, persons,
and places of its pages, and the deepest context for its doctrines. For
this ultimate end the Son of God shed his blood and poured out the
Spirit from on high, even to bring us into his Fathers house, in him,
as sons and daughters of God.

How lovely is your dwelling, O YHWH of hosts!
My soul longs, even faints, for the courts of YHWH,
My heart and flesh cry out with joy to the living God!
... How happy are those who dwell in your house,
   ever singing your praise!

                                    (Psalm 84:1-4)

*L. Michael Morales (PhD, Trinity College, University of Bristol) is Professor of Bib-
lical Theology at Greenville Presbyterian Theological Seminary. This chapter is the
prologue of his book* Who Shall Ascend the Hill of the Lord? A Biblical Theology
of the Book of Leviticus, New Studies in Biblical Theology Series, *(c) L. Michael
Morales 2015. Used by permission of InterVarsity Press, P.O. Box 1400, Downers
Grove, IL 60515, USA. www.ivpress.com.*

THE PROBLEM OF EVIL

by Benjamin Shaw

In a certain sense, evil is not a problem. It is an ordinary part of our everyday lives, whether at the natural level (witness floods and killer storms) or at the moral level (hatred, greed, lying, murder, theft). Even our most speculative writers do not seem to be able to imagine a world without evil. There is not a single piece of fiction in which evil is not crucial to the plot. Any number of examples can be drawn from the realm of speculative fiction and fantasy. In every case, sin and evil form the warp and woof of the story line. Evil is so ingrained in our universe, and in our perception of it, that we cannot imagine a universe without it.

Yet, in another sense, evil is a huge problem. The presence of evil is the issue with which atheists regularly attack Christians. "How can your God be all good, and all-powerful, and there be evil in the world?" In the view of the consistent atheist, of course, there is no evil. There is no moral law except that which is sociologically imposed. Yet even the atheist, inconsistently, considers many things evil in their very nature. The problem, of course, is more acute for the Christian, who believes that God is indeed good; that he is indeed sovereign. Yet, there is evil, not only in nature (natural disasters) but in the depths of the human soul. Everyone has the experience of doing that which he knows he ought not do. Everyone has the experience of being hurt by someone or something, and we know that such experiences have no better name than the name "evil." So, how is the problem to be dealt with? Is there an answer? If so, what is it?

It appears to me that there are three aspects to the answer. The first aspect we might call the philosophical or theological aspect. This is the aspect that I call *truth*. That is, the issue is what is true. The second aspect concerns the nature of God. This aspect I refer to as *glory*. The third aspect has to do with our perception of the experience of evil. It is, in some sense, aesthetic. So this I call *beauty*.

TRUTH

In this section, my approach is heavily dependent on the works of Francis Turretin, Charles Hodge, and especially Paul Helm. Turretin, in the opening lines of his treatment of providence and the problem of evil, calls it the most difficult question relating to the whole topic of providence. Paul Helm, in his book *The Providence of God* presents the issue in the form of a choice.[1] The following discussion is based primarily on Helm.

Is there risk, or is there no risk? Is God taking a chance or not? The traditional Arminian response to the problem of evil is that God took a risk in creating man as a free creature. If God were to make a creature that had an undetermined will, God would be taking a risk that the creature might choose to act against God, thus introducing evil into the creation. God did not know ahead of time what was going to happen when he thus created man with free will. Thus, the presence of evil in the world is a risked outcome. This is a very common Christian response to the problem of evil. Greg Koukl is a well-known Christian apologist who argues in this fashion.[2]

There are two problems with this answer. The first problem is that the Bible does not seem to be all that concerned about "free will" as the Arminian defines it. Instead, the Bible consistently presents man as "bound in sin and natures night."[3] It is the problem that Luther addressed in *The Bondage of the Will*, which was directed against Erasmus' free-will defense. Of course, that leaves the problem of Adams transgression, but that is a mystery for any approach to the problem. The second problem with the "free will" explanation is that it seems to lead inexorably to "openness theology." Openness theology is the view that God knows everything that can be known, but he

1   Paul Helm, *The Providence of God*, Contours of Christian Theology (Downers Grove: InterVarsity Press, 1993), 193-216.
2   See some of his discussions on his site "Stand to Reason" (www.str.org).
3   "And Can It Be," Charles Wesley.

does not, and cannot, know the future actions of free creatures. So while the gospel plan is put into effect, there can be no certainty on Gods part that any of his free creatures will in fact choose his gospel plan. Further, preaching and apologetics and prayer are all pointless, because there can be no such things as swaying an undetermined will.

A second approach to the risk-taking-God explanation is that of "middle knowledge" or Molinism, named after the sixteenth-century Jesuit Luis de Molina, who first proposed it. This is the view that, while God doesn't know the future actions of free creatures, yet he knows all possible worlds and chooses the one in which the benefits of the gospel are most widely spread. As with the Arminian explanation, however, there are two fundamental problems with Molinism. The first is that Molinism fails the Occam text. Occam's Razor is a philosophical axiom to the effect that the simplest explanation is probably the correct one. Molinism is unnecessarily complicated, making it less likely to be the correct explanation.[4] Further, Molinism as an explanation of the problem of evil suffers from the same fundamental weaknesses as does Arminianism - it doesn't comport with the Bible's presentation of the will of man, and it leads, if followed consistently, to openness theology. With both the Arminian explanation and the Molinist explanation any true sovereignty of God is lost. It is man who is, in effect, sovereign, at least with regard to the gospel.

Helm's third proposal is the Calvinist proposal: that God takes no risk in making a creature with the possibility, indeed the certainty, of sinning. The chief problem with this view is that appears to make God the author of sin. There are three elements to the response to this charge, plus an explanation of the meaning of this proposal. First, this view requires a correct definition of human freedom. That is, man does not have an undetermined will. Instead, it is argued, man is free to do as he pleases. The problem is that all man pleases to do is sin. Second, it raises the question of why Adam sinned. Adam was created perfect, but not immutable. Thus, mans state at the point of his creation was liable to change. This is a mystery, but at least it is a mystery shared by all versions of Christian theology. Third, God is

4 See the debate between Paul Helm and William Lane Craig on the issues at: https://www.youtube.com/watch?v=tZwywSLnJK4

not the author of sin, if that term is properly defined. Helm defines it as follows:

> He is not the author of it in the sense either that he is himself morally tainted by what he ordains, or that he takes away the responsibility of those creatures who perpetrate the evil.[5]

The question then arises as to what this explanation means with regard to the presence of sin. Or, to put it another way, why did God ordain sin, with all of the implications of that ordination? First, there is in this plan a greater display of God's glory and attributes than would have been possible without the presence of evil. Second, these things are fully displayed in the beauties of the plan of redemption. Third, these beauties are specifically displayed in the church. That is the assertion of Paul in Ephesians 3:8-10:

> To me, though I am the very least of all the saints, this grace was given, to preach to the Gentiles the unsearchable riches of Christ and to bring to light for everyone what is the plan of the mystery hidden for ages in God who created all things, so that through the church the manifold wisdom of God might now be made known to the rulers and authorities in the heavenly places.

These three things are well-expressed by Turretin.

> For if he had not permitted evil, his punitive justice would not have appeared, nor his pardoning mercy, nor the wisdom by which he turns evil into good, nor that wonderful love manifested in sending his son into the world for the salvation of the church.[6]

In short, God ordained evil for the display of his own glory and for the good of the church.

GLORY

In regard to this point, I want to turn to the book of Job. First, we

5 Helm, 196.
6 Francis Turretin, *Institutes of Elenctic Theology*, ed. James T. Dennison, Jr., trans. George M. Giger (Phillipsburg: P&R Publishing, 1992), Topic 6. Q. VII. Par. IX (p. 518).

need to note that evil in Job is not fundamentally a matter of natural evil, that is, such things as natural disasters. Instead, it is fundamentally a matter of moral evil. That there is natural evil is not disputed. But the Book of Job seems to presume the Genesis explanation of the origin of natural evil. Natural evil is the fruit of moral evil. It is because of the Fall of Adam that all of nature is plunged into vanity (see Romans 8:20-21).

Job's problem is that evil has made itself painfully present in his life. The Book of Job is frustrating for the reader, who knows what is happening, but Job and his friends do not. Jobs friends presume some horrific sin on the part of Job. Thus, much of what the friends say may be true in the abstract, but not true with regard to Job. The debates go on endlessly with no apparent solution to the problem. Finally, God himself appears out of the whirlwind, and the reader hopes that God will explain himself to Job. Instead, God seems to appear as the "cosmic bully," badgering Job with the unanswerable question, "Where were you?" As a result, many readers reach the end of the book frustrated, with the sense that none of the questions raised have been answered, or even addressed.

However, there is an answer hiding in the language of the book, but it takes some patience (perhaps the patience of Job) to dig that answer out.[7] For our purposes, we will focus on Job's initial complaint as that is set out in Job 3, and God's response in chapters 38-41. Job begins by cursing the day he was born. It is a reaction to his predicament that many understand. However, this is not just a wish that he had not been born. It is a curse on the day of his birth. This curse involves three elements, or three increasing levels of severity. The first is that the day become dark (vss. 1-10). It is not just a wish for nighttime rather than day. It is a wish for a return to primordial darkness. The second level is a wish for death (vss 11-19). And this is not present death but, as it were, retroactive death, that his entire life be undone, to end as he exits the womb. The third level of Job's curse is the worst. It is a resentment of light and life. There are, for example, five specific references to darkness in vss. 1-10. There are also four references either to the removal or the avoidance of light.

7 This portion of the discussion was suggested by, and depends on, Robert Alter, *The Art of Biblical Poetry* (New York: Basic Books, 1985), 85-110.

There is also the wish that even the hope of light be removed. Verses 20-26 also revisit the theme, emphasizing the resentment of life and light. Job's curse is, in short, a desire for the entire undoing of creation. The darkness he desires is the primordial darkness of Genesis 1:2, but without the life implied by the moving of the Spirit over the waters. Better that creation should never have taken place than that Job suffer as he is suffering. As Alter puts it: "The poetics of suffering in Chapter 3 seeks to contract the whole world to a point of extinction, and it generates a chain of images of enclosure and restriction."[8]

It is to this extremity that God responds in chapters 38-40. He does not address Job's complaint directly. He does not explicitly reject Jobs curse. Instead, he turns Job's curse on its head. Notice how Gods first words refer to the one who "darkens" counsel. God rejects Job's darkening as an act or wish born out of profound ignorance. God then moves on to deal in reverse order with the levels of Job's curse. He begins with the affirmation of creation, the very thing that Job wanted undone. And God affirms creation in the very terms of Job's complaint: life and light. What God is saying here is that all three go together. There is no creation without life and light. There is no un-creation without darkness and death. And then God adds one more element that is really a response to Job's suffering. God adds joy. That is the introduction to God's statement. And in the following four chapters, there is a frivolity, there is a lightness, there is a playfulness in God's rejoicing in his creation. Alter puts it this way:

> To be sure, the whole zoological section of the poem is meant to tell Job that God's tender mercies are over all His creatures, but tonally and imagistically this revelation comes in a great storm rather than in a still, small voice, for the providence portrayed is over a world that defies comfortable moral categorizings.[9]

In another place he says,

> The animal realm is a nonmoral realm, but the sharp paradoxes it embodies make us see the inadequacy of any merely human moral calculus - not only that of the friends, learned by rote, but even

8 Alter, 103-4.
9 Ibid., 104.

Job's, spoken out of the integrity of suffering.[10]

While that is profoundly true, the one element that Alter misses in his analysis is the element of joy. If one might say so, God shows his playfulness, his enjoyment, in his creation. In a book full of darkness and heaviness, it is God who brings in light and joy.

That Job has heard this is reflected in his final response to God in 42:5-6. The substance of Job's response is that now he knows God first-hand. Unfortunately, the beauty of Job's response is lost in the common translation of verse 6, reflected in the ESV (as well as most other English versions): "Therefore, I despise myself, and repent in dust and ashes." There are two major problems with this translation. First, the verb translated "despise myself" is not reflexive, that is, there is no "despise myself." It is, perhaps, commonly translated that way here because there is no direct object of the verb, so translators assume that Job is despising himself. But more commonly the verb means to reject. Again, there is no direct object to the verb, so what is Job rejecting? From the context (vs. 5), he is rejecting his previous second-hand knowledge of God, in favor of what he now sees. But the second half of verse 6 is also problematic. "Repent in dust and ashes" has become a common image for repentance. But again, of what does Job have to repent. God certainly does not charge him. In the following verses God speaks for Job, not against him. So we look again at the verb. Yes, it may mean repent. It may also mean to change one's mind, or to comfort oneself. Either of these is preferable to repent. If the former, Job's changing his mind is in parallel to his rejecting his former second-hand knowledge of God. If the latter, Job consoles himself upon (not in) dust and ashes. We need to remember that throughout the book (from the end of chapter 2) Job has been sitting on the ash heap. He is there still, but now, having seen God, having seen his glory, having seen, as it were, the joy of God in his creation, Job takes comfort in that beatific vision, though he remains upon the ash heap.[11]

It is in the vision of the glory of God that Job finds his consola-

10   Ibid., 102.
11   I am grateful to Dale Ralph Davis for this insight. See his *The Word Became Fresh* (Ross-shire, Scotland: Mentor, 2006), 118, fn 18.

tion. The suffering, the pain, the misunderstanding on the part of his friends all fade into insignificance now that Job has seen God.

BEAUTY

In 1934 Dorothy Sayers published the mystery novel *The Nine Tailors*. It featured her gentleman detective Peter Wimsey, but the story is not about Wimsey. Instead, it is a novel based on campanology or change-ringing. I ll let Sayers describe change-ringing.

> The art of change-ringing is peculiar to the English, and, like most English peculiarities, unintelligible to the rest of the world. To the musical Belgian, for example, it appears that the proper thing to do with a carefully tuned ring of bells is to play a tune upon it. By to the English campanologist, the playing of tunes is considered to be a childish game, only fit for foreigners; the proper use of bells is to work out mathematical permutations and combinations. When he speaks of the music of his bells, he does not mean musicians' music - still less what the ordinary man calls music. To the ordinary man, in fact, the pealing of bells is a monotonous jangle and a nuisance, tolerable only when mitigated by remote distance and sentimental association.... But what [the Englishman] really means is that by the English method of ringing with rope and wheel, each several bell gives forth her fullest and her noblest note. His passion - and it is a passionfinds its satisfaction in mathematical completeness and mechanical perfection, and as his bell weaves her way rhythmically up from lead to hinder place and down again, he is filled with the solemn intoxication that comes of intricate ritual faultlessly performed.[12]

In the book, campanology becomes a figure for providence, particularly regarding the various evils that occur in the course of the story. That use is particularly apt. Change-ringing, heard by the uninitiated, sounds like nothing but loud and objectionable noise, in fact, an awful lot of noise. But the reason it sounds like noise is because the person uninitiated in the art of change-ringing lacks both the understanding and the perspective necessary to appreciate it. I am told that

12   Dorothy Sayers, *The Nine Tailors* (New York: Harcourt Brace Jovanovich, 1962), 17-18.

an experienced campanologist, listening to a ring of bells, can tell both how many bells are being rung and also what particular method of change-ringing is being done. The uninitiated will hear only noise because he does not understand what is being done or why it is being done.

However awful change-ringing may sound to the uninitiated, it is not noise. Instead it is music. It is precise, it is careful, and it is, in its own way, beautiful. Change-ringing must be done with great care and precision, otherwise the exercise is ruined. I would suggest that the reader look up change-ringing on youtube.com to see, and hear, some examples. In order to appreciate change-ringing, however, the listener needs to learn, as it were, a different kind of music. As Sayers said, it is neither musicians' music nor what the ordinary man considers music.

As campanology produces a kind of music that is appreciated only by the initiated, so providence plays a tune that the ordinary man will not understand. To the ordinary man, providence, particularly when it comes to the matters of pain and evil, is only so much noise, painful in the experience, and painful to the heart. In order to appreciate the music of providence, we must learn a new kind of music, not human music but divine music. We must first learn the song of creation, that sung by the sons of God as they rejoiced in the creative work of God (Job 38:7). But that is not the only song we must learn. We must learn the song of Moses, the song of redemption foreshadowed. Though we no longer live under the Mosaic administration, we are still in the time of the "not yet." Our redemption draws nigh but it is not yet, in some sense, here. Finally, we must learn the song of the Lamb, redemption accomplished, applied, and completed (Revelation 15:3).

It is only in learning these songs, in learning this divine music, that we are then able to hear the music of the song of providence (including evil). As the country singer Garth Brooks put it, we will then be able to sing, "Our lives are better left to chance [providence]. I might have missed the pain, but then I'd have had to miss the dance."[13] It is because of the problem of evil that we, even in this life, begin to

13 Garth Brooks, "The Dance."

get a glimpse of the truth, of the glory, of the beauty of God, and we can sing his praise.

Benjamin Shaw (PhD, Bob Jones University) is the Academic Dean at Greenville Presbyterian Theological Seminary, and Professor of Old Testament and Hebrew. This paper is based on his "Just a Lot of Noise: Providence and the Problem of Evil," a lecture delivered at the 2014 Greenville Presbyterian Theological Seminary Spring Theology Conference.

PIETY: EXPERIMENTAL CALVINISM

by Ian Hamilton

Before we launch into our subject, I feel constrained to state what I hope is obvious - Calvinism is natively experimental. If it isn't, then it is not "Calvinism," however loudly it trumpets its adherence to the distinctive tenets of Calvinism. In other words, there is no such thing as "dead Calvinism." This is a theological oxymoron, and that for one simple reason: Calvinism claims to be biblical religion, and biblical religion is not only profoundly theological, it is also deeply experiential and engagingly affectional. Wherever men claim to be Calvinists, their lives and their ministries will pulse with life, the life of living, Spirit-inspired, Christ-glorifying, God-centered truth. This is the great feature of Calvins Institutes and Owens Works - they are instinct with life!

The question "What is Experimental Calvinism?" deserves, therefore, our deepest attention. In an age when the Church has been seduced by the mantra of modernity, there is a pressing need to recover the biblical gospel and re-assert with conviction and confidence those truths that gave birth to the Protestant Reformation.

Lest you be tempted to think this is little more than an in-house, "Reformed" debate, let me remind you that Benjamin Breckenridge Warfield argued in several of his writings that the very future of the Christian faith is inseparable from the fortunes of the Reformed faith.[1] Where God is not the pre-eminent focus of the Church, where mans enjoyment and not God's glory fuels the energies of the

---

1   *The Works of Benjamin B. Warfield* (1931; reprint, Grand Rapids, MI: Baker Book House, 1981), 5:353-369.

Church, where "programs" replace prayer, where sin is reduced to a personal and societal malfunction, it is not "Calvinism" that dies, it is the Christian faith itself!

Few of us would deny that what passes for Calvinism is often far removed from the passionately Trinitarian-centered, Christ-magnifying, Spirit-quickened, gospel-adoring, grace-humbling, obedience-loving religion of the Puritans. For many, sadly and tragically, Calvinism is characterized by little more than the Five Points. It is true that Calvinism is not less than the Five Points, but it is richly and profoundly more than the Five Points. I well recollect the first time I read John Owen. I was a young student travelling to an Inter-Varsity Conference in the Scottish Borders. As I read Owen on the mortification of sin, the thought gripped me, "This man knows my heart!" That is Calvinism. His exposition pulsed with life; indeed, the whole treatise breathed an atmosphere of life, - pulse-quickening, heart-engaging, mind-expanding life. This is what Warfield evidently was aiming to communicate when he said that the fountainhead of Calvinism does not lie in its theological system, but in its "religious consciousness." In other words, the roots of Calvinism are planted in a specific "religious attitude," out of which unfolds, as day follows night, a particular theology. He wrote, "The whole outworking of Calvinism in life is thus but the efflorescence of its fundamental religious consciousness, which finds its scientific statement in its theological system."[2] This is what so many miss in their assessment of, or espousal of, Calvinism. It is not first and foremost a theological system; it is more fundamentally a "religious attitude," an attitude that gives inevitable birth to a particular, precise, but gloriously God-centered and heart-engaging system of theology.

Let us now consider two aspects of experimental Calvinism, namely, the formative principle and the foundational experience.

THE FORMATIVE PRINCIPAL OF EXPERIMENTAL CALVINISM

What is the formative principle of Calvinism? Warfield was adamant that the "formative principle" of Calvinism is not what so many

2 Ibid., 5:354.

imagine - the doctrine of predestination - but the glory of the Lord God Almighty! So, the fundamental question posed in Calvinism is not "How can I be saved?" but "How shall God be glorified?" Experimental Calvinism is compellingly, rigorously, and joyfully theocentric. Paul's doxology in Romans 11:36, "For from Him and through Him and to Him are all things. To Him be the glory forever. Amen," is its pulse beat.

It was this passionate conviction that lay behind the longing of David Brainerd for God's glory as expressed in one of the last entries in his Diary:

> This day, I saw clearly that I should never be happy, yea, that God Himself could not make me happy, unless I could be in a capacity to 'please and glorify Him forever.' Take away this and admit me into all the fine havens that can be conceived of by men or angels, and I should still be miserable forever... Oh, to love and praise God more, to please Him forever! This my soul panted after and even now pants for while I write. Oh, that God may be glorified in the whole earth![3]

This is the authentic spirit of experimental Calvinism, and no one animated by such a spirit can be clinical or detached, far less cold and unfeeling.

What I am trying to say is simply this: "academic Calvinism" is a complete misnomer, a contradiction in terms. No man is a Calvinist merely because he has read Calvin or Owen, or the Shorter Catechism; or because he has digested Jonathan Edwards, or for that matter "the Doctor" (i.e., Martyn Lloyd-Jones), or any of the other great writers of the Reformed faith. One cannot be apprehended in any real sense by Gods majestic grace and gracious majesty and not be deeply, powerfully and permanently affected in the inner man. One may as well speak of a "living corpse!" What a challenge this ought to be to us! Do our lives and our ministries persuade others that we have been apprehended by God's majestic grace? Do they see and sense that the glory of God is the supreme passion of our lives?

3   *The Works of Jonathan Edwards* (1834; reprint, Edinburgh, Banner of Truth Trust, 1974), 2:381. The entry is for Lord's Day, July 26, 1746.

THE FOUNDATIONAL EXPERIENCE OF EXPERIMENTAL CALVINISM

In his excellent Banner of Truth booklet, *The Practical Implications of Calvinism*, Al Martin reminds us that no passage in Scripture more confronts us with "experimental Calvinism" than Isaiah 6, where we read of Isaiah's encounter with the living God - "the Lord" and "the King" - that so totally transformed his life that he was never the same again. His vision of the exalted, majestic, sovereign, and holy God overwhelmed him and shaped his existence. This is experimental Calvinism - it is the discovery that we are out of our depth (cf. Romans 11:33ff). Pastor Martin helpfully highlights the fundamental elements in Isaiah's encounter with the living God in the following manner.

First, Isaiah's encounter with God created a deep-felt awareness of his own sinfulness - "woe to me... I am ruined...!" When Isaiah saw God as he is, he was not left standing (far less dancing!), nor was he left proud and dispassionate; no, he was deeply humbled. There is little doubt that Isaiah already was a believing servant, but even so, he was somewhat of a stranger to the pulse-quickening sense of God's ineffable greatness. Isaiah was brought to see himself from God's vantage point. This is experimental Calvinism, when the revelation of the Lord shatters all of our fond, imagined notions about ourselves and brings us down to the dust! Isaiah saw what sin really is; namely, a serious affront to the glory and holiness of the almighty, majestic God that sets God against us (cf. Psalm 51:4). Experimental Calvinism is marked always by a deeply felt sense of sinfulness, and it cannot be otherwise! A genuine mourning over sin makes for fruitful spiritual soil, and no grace can flourish in any life that has not been and is not being, humbled by sin. If what we say about God and ourselves is truly what we believe, then Calvinists, of all people, have most to be humble about. Proud Calvinism, then, is another oxymoron!

Second, Isaiah's encounter with God brought about a new sense of Israel's corruption (v. 5). Isaiah's encounter with "the King" caused him to see through the fae of Israel's religion (cf. 1:10ff). Onlookers might perhaps have complimented Israel on the "healthy state" of its "religion." But when a man has had a sight of the majesty of God, he sees not only his own sinfulness, but the sinful state of his own generation, and particularly, of his own church. It was this conviction, no doubt, that spurred on Jonathan Edwards to deliver the heart-probing, biblical preaching that led, in part, to his dismissal from the pastorate in Northampton when his congregation would not face up to the true nature of their situation. It should be evident to all that this deep-seated awareness of sinfulness marks the prayers of Gods people in Scripture. Both Daniel and Nehemiah, to name but two, were constrained to pray, "Lord, we have sinned...!"

Third, Isaiahs encounter with God ingrained in him a deep, personal awareness of God's forgiving grace. As he was overwhelmed by his sinful uncleanness and "un-doneness," God mercifully sent an angel to bring him God's forgiving grace. The angel came with a live coal from the altar of sacrifice - a coal which symbolized the basis on which God forgives sinners - and he touched Isaiah's lips. Oh, how intense the pain of the searing and burning! However, with this pain came the cleansing of his soul and conscience, and a consecration of Isaiahs lips to speak forth God's word of truth. "Behold, this has touched your lips; and your iniquity is taken away, and your sin is forgiven" (v. 7). It is often asked, "What is so amazing about grace?" Perhaps the question stems from the lamentable fact that we have such little sense of the sinfulness of sin and the majestic holiness of God. Indeed, it appears that the word "grace" has almost altogether lost its true significance in the evangelical vocabulary. But if we truly come to see that the gulf between us and God is not a few short steps, but an infinite chasm, the cross and Gods grace will be our glory! To the forgiven sinner, forgiveness is a humbling, overpowering, captivating word. The chains of sin have been loosed, the burden of guilt has been removed, the stain of sin has been washed away, and there remains a deep sense of gratitude and indebtedness to the One that has brought about the liberation. Nowhere is this more clearly portrayed than in our Lords encounter with the "sinful woman" (Luke 7:47). The extravagance of her devotion to the Lord acutely embarrassed Simon the Pharisee, Jesus' host. Our Lord's response is one that ought to humble all of us: "He who is forgiven little, loves little." The depth of our love to the Savior is in proportion to the depth of our humble recognition of our sinfulness and our experience of and gratitude for his forgiving grace. Is it not true that many of us who call ourselves "Reformed" have lost the sense of the sheer wonder of sovereign grace? Before us is a truth to defend, a captivating, enrapturing truth to glory in.

Fourth, Isaiah's encounter with God caused him to yield his life unreservedly to the Lord Jehovah. "Here am I. Send me!" No cajoling and no pleading. Isaiah's response is that of a man to whom inexplicable, sovereign grace has come, the reflex action of a man who has "seen" the Lord and felt the power of his presence and grace. As has often been said, grace costs us nothing, but it demands everything! (cf. Matt. 8:18-22 and 10:37-39). This is experimental Calvinism. The story of William Borden of Yale wonderfully illustrates the point. Borden had long prepared to serve as a missionary in the Far East. He had been an outstanding student, with a passion for missions. After some years travelling throughout America calling young men "to go east and preach the gospel of Christ," he at last set sail himself for Burma. On reaching Alexandria, Egypt, however, he was struck down with cerebral encephalitis. He would never see Burma. As he lay dying he overheard someone saying, "What a waste." With the little energy he had, Borden replied, "No reserve! No retreat! No regrets!" This is the life of the experimental Calvinist. It is a life of unconditional surrender to the saving lordship of Jesus Christ.

Even when the Lord searchingly tested the reality of Isaiah's unconditional allegiance (vs. 9-10), Isaiah's reaction was striking. He did not say, " Thats not fair! Dont call me to such a grievous work!" No, he simply asked, "For how long, O Lord?" In other words, "You are God. You do as you please, for all you do is good and right and I am yours to do with as you please!" As Al Martin reminds us, "unconditionalism" in subjection to our Lord is one of the pulse beats of experimental Calvinism.

What can we say then? As we have already said, a "proud Calvinist" is a misnomer, an impossibility, for God alone is "the King" and he is "high and exalted" (cf. Isaiah 57:15). Again, to quote from Warfield, "There is nothing against which Calvinism sets its face with more firmness than every form and degree of autosoterism," that is, every form of self-salvation.[4] My daughter Rebecca, when she was fourteen years old, was asked by a teacher at school, "What is a Calvinist?" (Why she was asked that is another story.). She replied, "Calvinists believe that God saves sinners." You can perhaps imagine how moved and thankful my wife and I were to hear her say that. This truth is part of the reason why we state that Calvinism is nothing more nor less than biblical religion.

Ian Hamilton (DD, Greenville Presbyterian Theological Seminary) is a member of the Board of Trustees for Greenville Presbyterian Theological Seminary, and Adjunct Professor of Practical Theology. This chapter was taken and adapted from his longer treatment by the same name, found on pages 29-42 in Reformed Spirituality: Communing with Our Glorious God *(ed. Joseph A. Pipa, Jr. & J. Andrew Wortman), Taylors, SC (2003).*

4 *Works of Warfield*, 5:360.

CALVIN'S DOCTRINE OF VOCATION

by James E. McGoldrick

The term vocation comes from the Latin, *voco* which means "call." In Scripture it pertains to a divine summons to become part of God's people and to accept the responsibilities that entails. The Greek term *kaleo* too means a call or summons, and it, like the Hebrew *qāhal* refers to the people of God meeting for worship, that is, called together for that purpose. When the New Testament appeared in Greek *ekklēsia* became the name for a body of worshipers called together, as the word *klēsis* indicates.

Ek klēsis signifies people called out of ordinary pursuits to worship God and then to go forth into the world to serve him. In the epistle to the Hebrews (3:1) the members of this assembly are "partakers of a heavenly calling", which in 2 Timothy 1:9 is a "holy calling."[1] This *vocation* comes to all believers in Christ.

In 1 Corinthians 7:17-24, the Apostle Paul admonished his readers to understand that each one had received a calling/vocation with particular responsibilities to fulfil accordingly. In a striking manner he told Christians to accept the status God, in his providence, had assigned to them.

To some believers, that meant accepting the position of slaves, although he told them to accept freedom, if it became attainable. If emancipation does not occur, they need not fret, because "he who was called in the Lord while a slave, is the Lord's freeman" (I Cor. 7:22). In this context, calling signifies a status such as being married,

---

1 Unless otherwise noted, biblical texts are cited according to the NASB.

being circumcised, or living as a slave or a freeman, etc. Regardless of one's occupation or social standing, he or she is called to serve God.

In the apostolic and early post-apostolic era, Christians at times suffered persecution at the hands of Roman imperial officials, so they scorned some occupations as evil because people within them operated as agents of oppression and adherents to pagan religion. Sometimes the church required converts from paganism to renounce civil and military positions before receiving baptism.

After Emperor Constantine professed Christianity and granted official toleration to the church, Christians supported the imperial government gradually; and being a Christian gradually became a status symbol of social acceptance. Conditions of life improved considerably, but in this atmosphere of favor many church members became lax in zeal, even in morality. This led devout people to withdraw from society to form enclaves of committed believers who professed a special vocation to live in conformity to evangelical counsels, as in subscription to vows of poverty, chastity, and obedience. Those who retreated from the world valued the contemplative life of prayer and meditation over the active life of service to society. A sacred-secular dichotomy developed within Christian circles and gradually became a permanent feature of the developing ecclesiastical establishment.

The church in the Middle Ages often denigrated manual labor for wages as degrading, and it regarded those engaged in such toil as inferior people. Bernard of Clairvaux (1091-1153), for example) viewed monks as living on a higher plane than farmers, an idea which appears to reflect the enduring teaching of Pope Gregory I (c. 590-604), which exalted the contemplative life.

Eventually scholastic theologians came to realize that all Christians, regardless of occupation, are called to glorify God, and they may do so in so-called secular work. These scholars tried to connect vocation with secular pursuits, but in doing so they created a hierarchy of categories to assign comparative value to various occupations. Members of the clerical establishment stood at the top of the scale, with lesser occupations below them in descending order. The spiritual elite then had the highest calling.

There were perceptive thinkers who saw the error in denigrating the laity, but they continued to extol the clergy as though its members were the religious aristocracy in the kingdom of God.[2] This attitude conflicts sharply with the Apostle Paul's use of κλησις (*klēsis*) in 1 Corinthians 1:26-29. There he admonished his readers to "consider your calling, brethren, that there were not many wise according to the flesh, not many mighty, not many noble... so no man may boast before God." Every Christian receives an effectual call to salvation, and every Christian has a divinely ordained vocation to perform.

Although medieval writers discoursed about fulfilling the *counsels of perfection* within the clerical and monastic establishments, some earnest students of Scripture discovered a far broader and deeper meaning of vocation, one causally connected with the doctrine of divine providence. Among those who made this discovery, Martin Luther (1483-1546) was the pioneer; although a few preceding thinkers had been moving in the same direction. Luther associated vocation with God's creation and ordering of the world, that is, within his providence. Aside from the salvific call to embrace Christ as revealed in the Gospel, Luther directed Christians to focus their concerns on earth and the needs of God's creatures there. He saw vocation as a means to implement God's command to love one's neighbors, thereby to contribute to the proper ordering of society. Believers, in the exercise of their divinely bestowed talents, are agents of providence.

Rather than withdrawing from the world to seek salvation through works of piety, true Christians serve within the world by attending to the needs of others. All believers, regardless of their social standing, are to be engaged in fulfilling the duties of their priesthood, for all are members of the *sacred/spiritual estate*, and the contributions of one are not inherently superior to those of another.[3] To show his disdain for medieval teaching about vocation Luther wrote *The Judgment of Martin Luther on Monastic Vows*, in which he asked, "What would

2 Karl Holl, "The History of the Word Vocation," tr. by Helen F. Peacock, *Review and Expositor* 55 (1958), 127-40.
3 "The Judgment of Martin Luther on Monastic Vows," *Luther's Works*, tr. by James Atkinson (Philadelphia: Fortress Press, 1966), 44, pp. 245-400.

the monks and nuns do, if they heard that, in the sight of God, they are not a bit better than married people or mud-stained farmers?"[4]

Following the lead of Martin Luther, John Calvin too denied the traditional doctrine of vocation, and he contended the Roman Catholic exaltation of the monastic life had "set up a double Christianity" in which "hooded sophists" comprised a "conventical of schismatics disturbing the order of the church and cut off from the lawful society of believers."[5] Like Luther, Calvin denied emphatically that anyone could either obtain or maintain the spiritual perfection required by the so-called evangelical counsels which monks aspired to achieve. Calvin maintained a dynamic concept of God's providence as of a "watchful, effective sort, engaged in ceaseless activity..., governing heaven and earth... and he so regulates all things that nothing takes place without his deliberation."[6] Calvin discouraged speculation about God's essence and advocated that Christians study the divine character as revealed in Scripture, in order to please him. It is not profitable to be concerned about what God is "in himself." It is very beneficial, however, to focus on God "as he is toward us."[7]

There is not a trace of fatalism in this reformer's thinking. His firm affirmation of God's complete sovereignty did not incline Calvin toward resignation or indolence. It, on the contrary, motivated him to tireless activity in God's service. He rejected meaningless chance and mechanical determinism in favor of benevolent providence that gives meaning to history and calls humans to participate in the progress of God's kingdom on earth. He emphasized God's constant involvement with his creatures whose actions serve his sovereign purpose. Divine engagement with the elect is especially significant, and to them he has granted marvelous privileges, as they become knowing and willing collaborators in his design.

In his *Catechism of the Church of Geneva* (1545), Calvin declared the chief end of human life is "to know God by whom men were cre-

---

4   Ibid., 305.
5   John Calvin, *Institutes of the Christian Religion*, ed.by John T. McNeill, tr. By Ford Lewis Battles (Louisville: Westminster Press, 1966), IV.xiii.14.
6   Ibid, I.xiv.3.
7   Ibid., I.x.2; cf.III.ii.6.

ated... because he created us and placed us in this world...to be glorified in us.... Our life should be devoted to his glory."[8] This being so, all Christians must serve God obediently, and there can be no double standard, as when the medieval church required vows of complete obedience from its religious but did not expect that from laymen. Where the Roman Church assigned superior value and merit to ascetic withdrawal from the world, Protestants, Calvin prominent among them, emphasized living within society and there fulfilling the duties incumbent upon their various callings. Christians must be constantly aware that God "sustains, nourishes, and cares for everything he has made: even to the least sparrow."[9]

Calvin assigned such importance to the concept of vocation that he admonished believers to understand "the Lord bids each one of us in all life's actions to look to his calling.... He has appointed duties for every man in his particular way of life."[10] As a modern interpreter of the Reformation observed, all Christians have a calling "to share in the *opus Dei,* to mirror the work of the Creator in their work by establishing human relationships and in creating human community in response to God's affirmation of human life."[11] This being so, all honorable occupations are divine callings. It is an egregious error to regard people who perform ordinary jobs, doing only what is necessary for their survival, as being without vocations.[12]

Even unbelievers have vocations, although they are not aware of them. Their work, as well as that of the elect contributes to the orderly operation of providential arrangements, without which life could not continue. Christians perform the duties of their calling knowingly and willingly, while unbelievers do so in ignorance.[13] Christians must acknowledge the contributions of non-Christians and respect them as bearers of the *imago Dei,* even though sin has distorted that

---

8   John Calvin, "Catechism of the Church of Geneva," in *Calvin's Selected Works* II, tr. by Henry Beveridge (Grand Rapids: Baker Book House, 1983 rpt. of 1849 edn) p. 37.

9   Calvin, *Institutes,* I.xvi.1.

10   Ibid., III.x.6.

11   Iain Nicol, "Vocation and the People of God," *Scottish Journal of Theology* 33 (1980), 372.

12   Ibid., p. 365.

13   Emil Brunner, *The Divine Imperative,* tr, by Olive Wyon (Philadelphia: Westminster Press), p. 221. Although hostile toward Calvin's view of theology proper, Brunner expressed appreciation for his concept of Vocation.

image. They are nevertheless neighbors. In explaining the parable of the Good Samaritan, Calvin said Jesus taught "the word 'neighbor' extends indiscriminately to every man, because the whole human race is united by a sacred bond of fellowship."[14] Christians must regard as neighbors even those who hate them.[15]

In addition to their calling to become disciples of Christ, believers receive other callings relative to the positions they hold in God's providential order for their lives. In all relationships, they must implement the requirements of stewardship, whether they be engaged as employees, employers, spouses, parents, church members, citizens, etc. Being a husband, for example, obligates a man to assist his wife in daily domestic chores, even rising in the middle of the night to attend to a crying infant. Husbands and wives are to be mutually submissive, as circumstances require them to be. Here the "law of love" must govern their attitudes and actions.[16]

In their role as subjects/citizens, their vocation requires God's people to obey, respect, and support civil rulers, even when those officials are unjust. This is not a demand for unqualified obedience, since civil rulers may order their subjects to sin, in which case, disobedience becomes a moral responsibility, a duty incumbent upon their vocation.

John Calvin believed the faithful performance of one's vocation glorifies God and benefits both society and the person who is faithful. He urged Christians to consider occupations "which yield the greatest advantage to one's neighbors."[17] Since believers need not work for salvation, they are free to dedicate themselves to serving others, and that includes all kinds of people, regardless of their social standing or their faith or lack thereof. As Calvin put this matter, "we ought to embrace the whole human race without exception in a single feeling of love."[18]

14 John Calvin, *Commentary on a Harmony of the Evangelists III* tr, by William Pringle (Grand Rapids: Baker Books, 2000 rpt.) p. 61.
15 John Calvin, *Commentary on the Epistles of Paul to the Galatians and Ephesians*, tr. by William Pringle (Grand Rapids: Baker Books, 2009 rpt.), pp. 160-1.
16 John Calvin, *Commentary on the Catholic Epistles*, tr. by John Owen (Grand Rapids; Baker Book House, 2009 rpt.), pp. 147-8.
17 Calvin, *Commentary on Ephesians*, p, 300. There is a summary of Calvin's teaching about the role of various callings in *Institutes*, II,viii.46.
18 Ibid., II.viii.55.

The elect are "justified not without works, but not through [by] works," and their vocation is the fruit of their election. The sign of vocation is faith, but the sign of faith is sanctification, that is, good works. The elect will display "a passion to bear fruit in transforming service to all mankind."[19] Regardless of how obviously depraved people may be, Christians are obliged to seek their welfare through the ministry of charity. As Calvin remarked, God "bids us to extend to all men the love we bear to him, that this may be an unchanging principle: whatever the character of the man, we must yet love him because we love God."[20]

In Geneva, this concern led to the practice of special ministries to sick people, prisoners, elderly and infirmed residents, even to foreigners who had fled there to escape persecution in Catholic lands. Officials of church and state considered themselves co-workers with God to support his purpose for the benefit of needy people.[21] They viewed this work as their vocation. Calvin urged Genevan Christians to realize there was nothing they could do for God, who is self-sufficient. He told them therefore, "since then your generosity cannot extend to him [God], you must practice it toward the saints on earth."[22]

Calvin, as indicated above, did not restrict the ministry of charity to the saints alone. He understood humanity's most urgent need is, not for physical health and sustenance, but for eternal salvation. Humanitarian aid is not enough. As one modern Calvinist put it, the inadequacy of such assistance is "it alleviates, but it fails to redeem."[23] Whether or not the ministry of charity leads to conversion of lost people, Calvin maintained the Christians' duty is the same. He wrote, "though there are many that are undeserving, while others abuse our liberality, we must not on this account leave off helping those that

19   Ray C. Petry, "Calvin's Conception of the *Communio Sanctorum*," *Church History* 5 (1936), 231.
20   Calvin, *Institutes*, II.viii.55.
21   See Petry, "Calvin's Conception," and the following essays by Robert M. King dom: "Social Welfare in Calvin's Geneva," *American Historical Review* 76 (1971), 50-69; and "Calvinism and Social Welfare," *Calvin Theological Journal* 17 (1982), 212-30.
22   Calvin, *Institutes*, III,viii.5.
23   J.G. Matheson, "Calvin's Doctrine of the Christian Life," *Scottish Journal of Theology* 2 (1947), 53. This is a rather critical appraisal of Calvin's thinking, but one which duly recognizes his great contributions.

need our aid."[24]

One class of people well able to participate in charity were the merchants of Geneva, whose vocation, Calvin said, was an honorable one when they conducted trade honestly and thereby performed a valuable service to the community. Since Geneva was a haven for persecuted Protestants, its merchants had many opportunities to help them. As their pastor, Calvin associated with them and with people of all occupations, guiding them in the matter of their social responsibilities, thereby fulfilling their vocational duties.[25] Calvin noted how important work diligently performed is to a healthful economy, and he taught that such labor is part of the creation God intended to continue always, even if the fall had not occurred. In spite of the fall, those who toil honorably will find joy and satisfaction in their labor. Calvin cited Psalm 8:6-8 to show God's providential arrangement for humans to be his vicegerents in developing the assets of the earth — a task which requires continuous work.[26]

In his providence, God arranges the circumstances that determine the callings he has ordained for his creatures, and he equips them with the necessary talents to perform them. Realizing this is so, Calvin and other Protestant reformers promoted education for all classes of people, so all be prepared to accept their calling to work for God's glory.[27] In Calvin's judgment "ignorance of providence is the ultimate of all miseries, and the highest blessedness lies in the knowledge of it."[28] This is especially relevant when, in the pursuit of their callings, believers encounter cruel opposition and must suffer for their loyalty to Christ, Calvin urged confidence that God has made the care of his people his personal concern.

In accord with other Protestant reformers, Calvin rejected the secular

24   John Calvin, *Commentaries on the Epistles of the Apostle Paul to the Philippians, Colossians, and Thessalonians,* tr. by John Pringle (Grand Rapids: Baker Book House, 2009 rpt.), pp. 358-9.
25   Georges A. Barrois, "Calvin and the Genevans," *Theology Today* 21 (1965), 458-65 a helpful study of the reformer's relations with the various classes of Genevan society.
26   Jack Buckley, "Calvin's View of Work," *Radix* 15 (1984), 8-12; 28. A splendid treatment of vocation is that of Gene Edward Veith, Jr., *God at Work* (Wheaton, Ill., Crossway Books, 2002).
27   Ibid., 17-21.
28   Calvin, *Institutes,* I.xvii.11.

humanism of Italian Renaissance scholars, with their emphasis on self- esteem and material rewards for their achievements. The Protestant rebuttal featured the insistence that God determines how and where humans are to serve him. Rather than regard vocation as only a human choice of occupations, the reformers stressed the role of divine calling which is sometimes contrary to human choice. Where the humanists stressed personal choice, the reformers emphasized divine mandates.

Luther and Calvin sought to provide at least elementary instruction for everyone, as they realized implementation of the priesthood of all believers required literacy.[29] The extension of education to the public at large came as Protestant churches, often with support from civil rulers, established schools for every level of instruction. One of the most enduring contributions of the Reformation to the modern world is availability of education to all socio-economic classes.

The Protestant doctrine of vocation, derived from a proper appreciation for divine providence, has exerted substantial influence upon the economic development of the modern world through its concept of the work ethic. The Protestants sanctified all occupations performed for God's glory, and thereby they elevated even menial tasks to a status of honor and dignity. Calvin in particular urged Christians to discard selfish ambition and quest for fame and to focus on pleasing God through conscientious performance of the work their Lord had prescribed in granting them the privileges of their respective vocations.[30]

Although Calvin was not an economic theoretician and so did not present a systematic program for economic development, he encouraged the ethical growth of commerce and industry in Geneva, and his disciples in France, the Netherlands, and elsewhere became leaders in those enterprises. Calvin stressed the sanctity of private property, and he approved the practice of usury, but only as regulated by the

29 Coverage of this matter appears in Douglas, "Talent and Vocation," and in James Edward McGoldrick, "John Calvin: Erudite Educator," *Mid-America Journal of Theology* 21 (2010), 121-32. A convenient collection of Luther's writings on education is F.V.N. Painter (ed.), *Luther on Education* (St. Louis: Concordia Publishing House, 1928).

30 See Michael Monheit, "The Ambition for an Illustrious Name: Humanism, Patronage, and Calvin's Doctrine of Calling," *Sixteenth Century Journal* 23 (1992), 267-89 for an excellent study of this topic.

state so as to prevent exploitation of the poor. He did not endorse the *laissez-faire* philosophy now associated with Adam Smith (1732-90) and his free market treatise *The Wealth of Nations* (1776), the work of a humanist who assumed the inherent goodness of human nature. The decline of the work ethic in modern times has occurred as even Christians have discarded the Reformation view of vocation and have detached their daily employment from their relationship to God. The effect of this detachment has been the denigration of humans while people ignore the claims of God.[31]

In early modern Europe, as some church members became prosperous, many lost the sense of calling to serve and instead saw vocation as the pursuit of upward social mobility rather than a summons to charity toward their neighbors.

Among Protestant reformers of the sixteenth century, there was unanimous subscription to the priesthood of all believers, so Calvin's view was not exceptional, but he understood clearly the connection between this precious truth and its relevance for ordinary work Christians perform. This reformer regarded all work as a religious activity, and he maintained that everyone should work, even those who do not need the income from wages. Working is a divine command, and those who do not need the income from their labors can use it to aid people in distress.

Calvin was emphatic in denouncing idleness.[32] He therefore warned sternly: "We are God's; let his wisdom and will... rule all our actions.... [C]onsulting our self-interest is the pestilence that most effectively leads to our destruction."[33] Believers must never therefore regard commerce, politics, education, etc. as autonomous domains separated from religion. No area of life is secular, and work is an

---

31 For further information about Calvin's view of economics, see C. Gregg Singer, "Calvin and the Social Order," in *John Calvin, Contemporary Prophet*, ed. By Jacob R. Hoogstra, (Grand Rapids: Baker Book House, 1959), pp. 227-41; Donnio Walters, "The Reformation and Transformation of Western Culture," *Journal of Christian Reconstruction* 2 (1975), 109-14.

32 The entire matter of Calvin's concern for the social responsibilities of the Christian life has received thorough examination in André Bieler, *Calvin's Economic and Social Thought*, ed. by Edward Dommen, tr. by James Grieg (Geneva: World Alliance of Reformed Churches, 2005). A briefer study by the same author is *The Social Humanism of Calvin*, tr. by Paul T, Fuhrmann (Richmond, Va.: John Knox Press (1964).

33 Calvin, *Institutes*, III.vii.1.

honor, not a necessary evil to be endured. It is a visible way to display the reality of one's saving faith.

One of the great tragedies of modern times is the tendency, even among Christians, to regard providence as operating only in exceptional events. As this assumption has gained acceptance, a corresponding loss of confidence in divine sovereignty has become evident. Without firm belief in providence, life is without meaning; and history is just a meaningless series of incidents and accidents. As Shakespeare phrased it, "Life is a tale, told by an idiot, full of sound and fury, signifying nothing." The biblical cure for this pernicious malady calls all Christians to receive God's call with gratitude and to perform the duties of their respective vocations with the goal of pleasing their Savior, who has commanded them, "Let your light shine before men in such a way that they may see your good works and glorify your Father who is in heaven" (Matthew 5:16). Yes, God is still calling all Christians.[34]

James E. McGoldrick (PhD, West Virginia University) is Professor of Church History at Greenville Presbyterian Theological Seminary. This chapter was adapted from his "Calling All Christians! Calvin's Doctrine of Vocation," in The Scottish Bulletin of Evangelical Theology, *Volume 34, No. 2, Autumn 2016. Used by permission.*

34 A biographical essay which deals with some of the features of Calvin's thinking about vocation is James Edward McGoldrick, John Calvin, Theologian of Head, Heart, and Hands." *Scottish Bulletin of Evangelical Theology* 29 (2011), 177-95. For a modern explanation of the decline of confidence in divine providence, see Langdon B. Gilkey, "The Concept of Providence in Contemporary Theology," *Journal of Religion* 43 (1963), 171-92.

THE CHURCH'S
EVANGELISTIC MISSION

by L. Anthony Curto

From its very beginning, the church of God has been evangelizing for her Lord and Savior. For millennia, the disciples have been going to the nations with the good news of redemption. It seems to be second nature—to evangelize is like breathing. We don't need to think about it or analyze it. We just need to do it. But, sadly, the church struggles in its evangelistic task. Why is that?

In the spring of 2006, I had the privilege of working with the OPC mission to Haiti. I had gone there to help train men for leadership in the new and growing work on Lagonav. I was staying with the Baugh family in Kalico. The area is a barren and rocky portion of Haiti outside of Port-au-Prince. One morning as we were leaving, I noticed a group of about ten men working to clear a field of rocks so they could plant watermelons. That seemed to me to be a terribly difficult task. You see, the field was littered with thousands of rocks in various sizes and shapes.

Later in the day, when we returned, the men were gone. There were a few piles of rock in various places around the field, but there were still thousands of rocks that needed to be removed.

This scenario continued for several days, but each day the number of workers diminished. Finally, on the fifth day, there were no workers at all in the field as we left in the morning. I asked someone why the men were not working. The response I received was startling: "The rocks have won!" The men had given up. The rocks were too numerous, and the labor was too hard.

That night, as I lay on my bed thinking about the difficulties of those poor farmers, I realized that their physical struggle to clear a field is much like our spiritual struggle to do the work of evangelism. We start off to the field to do our work, only to have the "rocks" win. So many rocks stand in the way that we become discouraged and give up. Even more difficult is the fact that the rocks are not only around us, but also in us. Because of this, true biblical evangelism is either neglected or compromised.

Some of those rocks are there because of our unbelief. Many people struggle with the rock of unbelief in the supernatural. They live with their thoughts and lives consumed by this world. In so doing, they forget, become blinded to, or simply ignore the spiritual state of multitudes lost in sin. They harden themselves against thoughts of coming judgment and live as if only the present matters. They live as if there is no world to come.

Others struggle with the rock of unbelief in the power of God. God has been rendered powerless by the technologies and science of this age, they think. God may have been powerful in ages past, but he has been thwarted in his purposes by the advances of human ingenuity. After all, this is the age of postmodernism.

Still others struggle with the rock of unbelief in the gospel. What does the world need? Some answers commonly given include: education, political stability, growing economies, and medical advances. Can the gospel, the simple teaching of and about Christ, really make a difference in the world? Is it truly "the power of God for salvation to anyone who believes"? Some, while believing it for themselves, do not believe that it would have much impact on the world in which we live.

Many fall at the rock of faithlessness. They have no zeal for the glory of God. Forgetting from where they have come and seeing no vision for the glory of God, they retreat into a mundane pattern of life. Life, like the ever-rolling stream, leads them away, doing little or nothing for the advancement of Christ's kingdom.

The Necessity of Evangelism

The church must evangelize. She has received a commission from our Lord and Savior to evangelize all the nations of the world. Several passages of Scripture come to mind: Matthew 28:16-20, Mark 16:15-16, Luke 24:44-49, Acts 1:6-8, and Romans 10:5-15. Each of these passages clearly demonstrates that the church is to do the work of evangelism.

There is more here also. It must be realized, on the basis of Christ's instruction, that the church is to be a proselytizing institution, and, by implication, that the church, without evangelizing, will not long continue to exist. In other words, spiritual procreation is by evangelization. The church that does not do the work of evangelism dies. The church that forsakes propagating the good news becomes a relic of the past. The issue here is not whether a church is strong or weak, but whether it is alive or dead.

There is another point to be gleaned from these passages concerning the necessity of evangelism, and that is that without an evangelizing church there is no hope for the lost. How will the lost know on whom to call, unless they are told? Who is to tell them? The answer is: an evangelizing church. For these reasons, we should realize that evangelism is not optional, but indispensable.

The Necessity of Reformed Evangelism

What I am endeavoring to do here is not to set before you a generic, one-size-fits-all kind of evangelism. There is much confusion today as to what evangelism is, how it is to be conducted, and by whom. I believe that much of this confusion has been caused by the promoting of generic evangelism. We want to have a God-centered, God-glorifying evangelism. To do so, our evangelism must be biblically and theologically informed. That is what a generic, one-size-fits-all evangelism cannot be. In fact, the more one seeks to make his evangelism generic, the less informed it will be, and to that extent it will not be God centered and God glorifying.

So what is Reformed evangelism? Reformed evangelism is the proclamation of Jesus Christ, in the power of the Spirit, to sinful men in order that they may come to put their trust in God through him, and receive him as their Lord and serve him as their King in the fellowship of his church (I owe this definition to RE Mark Bube).

Space does not allow me to open up this definition fully at this time. Therefore, I will limit my remarks in this article to the agent of the evangelistic enterprise.

THE AGENT OF EVANGELISM

Scripture teaches that Christ has ordained the church to be his agent in evangelism (Matt. 28:16-20). The church has been endowed by Christ with his spirit (Acts 2), his word (2 Tim. 3:16), his ministry (Eph. 4:8-16), and his ordinances (Matt. 28:16-20). The universal, visible church is Christ's instrument for the spread of his kingdom to all nations. To fulfill this task, our Savior has constituted his church as an organism (his body, his bride) and as an organization or institution (his kingdom, his household, and his temple). When we speak about the church doing evangelism, we look at the task from one of these two perspectives.

In evangelism, the church shows forth, demonstrates, or announces the lordship of Christ to the watching world. He has given to the church, as an organization, the word to preach and the sacraments to administer. The ascended Lord Jesus has so gifted the church, that it can utilize its gifts to accomplish its task of taking the gospel to the ends of the earth. When the church sends forth preachers with the word and the sacraments, Christ's kingdom will be established as a city set on a hill, shining forth a light to all those who sit in darkness (Rom. 10:14-17).

Too often, Christians forget this aspect of evangelism. The church, as the covenanted community of believers under the lordship of Christ, its head, is the appointed agency to send preachers around the world, beginning at home and going to every nation, kindred, tribe, and tongue.

Having said this, we must not think that sending preachers and missionaries to evangelize exhausts the church's obligation to spread the good news. Far from it! The church is not only a well-ordered society, but also the living body of Christ. The church, as his body, in union with its head, is a living organism, designed to show forth the praises of him who has called her out of darkness into his marvelous light (1 Pet. 2:9).

This is the perspective that the apostle Paul has in mind when he reminds the believers at Philippi that, as children of God, they are to shine as lights in the midst of a perverse and crooked nation (Phil. 2:15). This will be accomplished as they hold fast to the word of life (Phil. 2:16). The apostle Peter exhorts the believers of Asia Minor to do this also, in 1 Peter 3:15: *But in your hearts regard Christ the Lord as holy, always being prepared to make a defense to anyone who asks you for a reason for the hope that is in you.*

Here Peter exhorts the church to carry out a twofold task. Christians are to sanctify Christ in their hearts, and they are to give a defense (a positive presentation, a testimony) for the hope that is within them.

The church fulfills this task as his body, both corporately and individually. Corporately, this is accomplished as the body displays the lordship of Christ (sanctifying the Lord) in their life as believers (Eph. 5:1; 4:25; 4:1; John 13:35), in their unquestioned obedience to the word of God as their only rule of faith and practice, in their uncompromising opposition to evil and the kingdom of Satan (Mic. 6:8), and in their full-orbed worship of God in spirit and truth (John 4:23-24).

As the church corporately sanctifies Christ in her midst, so must each individual Christian. To be a witness (one who gives a positive presentation, a testimony) for Christ, one's life must display the lordship of Christ. To do so, one must hold fast to the word of life (Phil. 2:12; Gal. 5:22-24). The lordship of Christ will be evident in the Christian's life. It will be evident because his or her life will be one of faith, humility, love, boldness, joy, and patience. In this way, the witness (positive presentation, testimony) will not come in word only, but in truth and life.

Evangelism can never be cut off from that which the Lord has provided for its accomplishment. As we saw, he has given his spirit, his word, his ministry, and his church as resources for the task of evangelism. To do evangelism without these resources is like trying to propel a canoe without paddles.

MOBILIZATION FOR EVANGELISM

One of the most frequently asked question I hear is, "How do you mobilize and motivate a congregation to do biblical evangelism?" This is an important question. In answering it, the first point to be made is that God himself is the great mobilizer and motivator of his church. Now this might seem to be a trite or pietistic response, but it is true. The psalmist states, "Unless the Lord builds the house, those who build it labor in vain. Unless the Lord watches over the city, the watchman stays awake in vain" (Ps. 127:1). The application of this truth to mobilizing and motivating a congregation to evangelize is obvious. Unless God is behind our effort in evangelism or in our efforts to marshal his church in this spiritual battle, we are laboring in vain.

How does God call his church to the work of evangelism? To answer this question, let us look at the account of Isaiah's call and commission to the work of evangelism in Isaiah 6:1-9. In this account, we see Isaiah go from a man who cries "Woe is me, I am lost," to a man who shouts, "Here am I! Send me." What caused this metamorphosis, this transformation in Isaiah? God gave to Isaiah a vision of the glory of his person, a taste of the glory of his work, and a passion for the glory of his message.

We could spend much time looking at these, but for our purposes let us note three things. First, the vision of the glory of God's person as the sovereign Lord humbled the prophet. Isaiah saw himself for what he was. Without God, he was a man without hope, helpless and undone. The Lord and the Lord alone is the sovereign King. God is holy, high and lifted up, and men are completely dependent upon him for all things. Only God can save and bring deliverance.

Second, the taste of the glory of God's work raised the prophet up. He was renewed and made alive. The guilt of his sin was removed, and he was made a new man. He saw the excellence of God as his Savior. He realized that God's favor and acceptance were not found in himself, but in God's grace and love for sinners. Only the Lord can raise those who are spiritually dead. And when God gives life, he gives it to the full. For Isaiah, all things had become new.

Third, the message of God influenced him and made him zealous and passionate for the cause of God. Wrath and judgment were coming. The wrath of God is a consuming fire. Nothing would be left. All would be destroyed in God's vengeance and anger. Yet the Lord would bring forth a shoot from the stump of Jesse (Isa. 11:1), a branch in which all may seek refuge. There is no other place of safety. In this place, all who seek refuge shall be secure. The Branch is all-glorious—the pride and honor of all the earth (Isa. 4:2).

In that way, God motivated Isaiah to shout, "Here am I! Send me" (Isa. 6:8). And it is in this way that those who are called by God today to lead his church must mobilize and motivate the people of God for the work of evangelism. If the church is going to respond to its call to spread the gospel to all nations, it must have a vision of the glory of God's Christ, the Son of God, who in the plan of God came and died for sinners, elected by the Father. The church must see Christ in his glorious session at the right hand of God, who through his spirit is subduing the nations. God's work in Christ is full and complete. The message of the gospel must therefore be proclaimed to every creature.

L. Anthony Curto (DMin, Westminster Seminary California) is Associate Professor of Applied Theology in Missions and Apologetics at Greenville Presbyterian Theological Seminary. This chapter was reprinted from New Horizons, *February 2009. Used by permission.*

HONORING CHRIST IN CHURCH COURTS
Proverbs 15:1-4
by Ryan McGraw

It is important to be mindful both of what we say in church courts and how we say it. As John Kitchen wrote, "Speech has the potential to quiet a riot or to fan the embers of anger (Prov. 12:18; 15:18; 25:15)."[1] Proverbs 15:1-4 can set healthy parameters around how we should conduct ourselves in debates in church courts. On this side of glory, Christians, including presbyters, often display a mixture of both models. While through sanctification of the Spirit we shine in Christ from one degree of glory to another (2 Cor. 3:18), we can often unintentionally set our light under a basket by shading it through indwelling sin in our speech.

The burden of this essay is to show in light of Proverbs 15:1-4 that we must learn, as presbyters, so to moderate our speech as to honor Christ and to edify his church. Doing so will enable us better to promote the glory of our Savior and the peace and purity of the church. In order to explain and to illustrate these principles, I have extracted the parts of Prov. 15:1-4 into a list of positive exhortations and negative injunctions, highlighting distinctly the principle of accountability found in verse three. Since no man spoke as Christ did (Jn. 7:46), and because the Pharisees condemned themselves out of their own mouths (Jn. 9:41), both examples are useful to illustrate vividly the principles taught in this text. This article concludes with some directions designed to help presbyters speak well in church courts.

---

1   John A Kitchen, *Proverbs: A Mentor Commentary* (Fearn, Ross-shire: Mentor, 2006), 325. Kitchen will serve as a useful and simple guide to this passage throughout the material below.

SPEECH TO CULTIVATE

A soft answer turns away wrath (v. 1)[2]

Cultivating a "soft answer" is vital in promoting the church's well-being. It is not enough to be right. We must cultivate what Kitchen calls, "a conciliatory tone." A "soft" or "gentle" answer yields great fruit. Kitchen notes, "A 'gentle answer" can quench even white hot anger."[3] All of the principles given in Proverbs 15:1-4 presuppose disagreement among the parties involved. What would a Presbytery or a General Assembly be without healthy disagreement and debate? This is not wrong in itself, but it can be either helpful or hurtful depending on how we conduct ourselves as presbyters. Remember that "With patience a ruler may be persuaded, and a soft tongue will break a bone" (Prov. 25:15).

The tongue of the wise commends knowledge (v. 2)

This proverb concerns the form of our speech more directly. How we say what we say is as important as what we say. This strengthens the point made by verse one. It includes when we speak, what words we use, and our tone of voice.[4] Sometimes it is not the right time to speak. We can apply this principle by fully hearing out others' arguments before responding to them. Our words must always be full of wisdom as well. This involves saying the right thing, at the right time and in the right way. Even Jesus grew in wisdom and stature and in favor both with God and men (Lk. 2:52).

We may, however, speak at the right time and use the right words, but say them with the wrong tone. Remember the biblical adage, "Even a fool who keeps silent is considered wise; when he closes his lips, he is deemed intelligent" (Prov. 17:28). While we cannot remain silent over moral issues, we should consider both how we speak to issues and whether we are in a fit state do so wisely. You may need to speak regardless of these considerations, but sometimes it would be better to let someone in a better state of mind do it instead. Remember that

2   Unless otherwise noted, all Scripture citations are taken from the English Standard Version.
3   Kitchen, *Proverbs*, 325.
4   Ibid.,326.

our aim is Christ's glory through the peace and the purity of His church. Whether or not we communicate wisely can help or hinder these goals.

A gentle tongue is a tree of life (v. 4)

A "gentle tongue" is a "soothing" tongue. This verse adds the idea that a gentle tongue has healing power. A parallel to the Hebrew text is Jer. 8:15: "We looked for peace, but no good came; for a time of healing, but behold, terror."[5] Our speech in church courts should aim to heal divisions rather than to justify them on the pretense of a good cause.

The outcome of a gentle or healing tongue is a clear allusion to the Tree of Life from the Garden of Eden. While the angel with the flaming sword teaches us that man can never regain access to the Tree of Life through keeping the covenant of works, Christ both merits and purchases for us the promise embodied by the tree (Rev. 22:2). In relation to our text, however, this reminds us of Jesus' warning that by our words we will be justified and by our words we will be condemned (Matt. 12:37). In theological terms, this entails the justification of our works rather than that of our persons (Jas. 2:17-18). Nevertheless, such good works are found in the way to life.[6] In the context of Proverbs, Kitchen reminds us that wisdom of speech (Prov. 3:18)[7] is related organically to righteousness of life (Prov. 13:12).[8] Life results from right desires and hopes, which stem from right faith and practice (e.g., Ps. 37:3-6).

Healing words can promote life to others as well.[9] Surely this is part of what Paul had in view when he wrote, "Keep a close watch on yourself and on the teaching. Persist in this, for by so doing you will

5   Ibid., 327.
6   See Westminster Confession of Faith 16.2 and 6.
7   "She is a tree of life to those who lay hold of her; those who hold her fast are called blessed."
8   "Hope deferred makes the heart sick, but a desire fulfilled is a tree of life." See Kitchen, *Proverbs*, 327.
9   Kitchen, *Proverbs*, 327.

save both yourself and your hearers" (1 Tim. 4:16). Personal godliness and sound doctrine are inseparable twins.

ILLUSTRATIONS FROM CHRIST

Christ is both the foundation of our justification and the pattern of our sanctification. This includes our speech, even when dealing with others who are in error or who simply disagree with us. Before raising Lazarus, Jesus dealt gently with Martha by responding with the right words, at the right time, and in the right way, even when she implicitly questioned his actions and motives (Jn. 11:21-27). Jesus answered her gently and he wept with her and her family (Jn. 11:35). When His disciples found it unthinkable for Him to go away, even though it proved necessary for their salvation and for ours, Jesus explained what He was doing and how to follow Him (Jn. 14:1-11), what they should do after He left (v. 12-14), and how the Spirit would enable them to do it (v. 15-31). Upon his ascension into heaven, when His disciples still fostered false hopes that Christ would liberate the nation of Israel from the Romans, He patiently told them that such things were not for them to know, but that they must wait for the coming of the Spirit (Acts 1:6-8).

Jesus urged the multitudes, "Come to me, all who labor and are heavy laden, and I will give you rest. Take my yoke upon you, and learn from me, for I am gentle and lowly in heart, and you will find rest for your souls" (Matt. 11:28-29). If Christ spoke so wisely in the midst of such confusion, then let us imitate his soft answer, wise speech, and life-giving words in our labors in church courts. Let us not make church courts laborious and our fellow presbyters heavy laden.

SPEECH TO AVOID

But a harsh word stirs up anger (v. 1b)

To face the facts, Presbytery and Assembly debates can become tense. All of us have likely been guilty at some point of imputing motives to others or of assuming the worst outcome at a meeting. Pregnant suspicions and emotions often give birth to harsh words. Kitchen observes, "Unguarded words escalate any ill will that may be already present."[10] While wise words are designed to promote debate and to add clarity to issues, harsh words are designed to wound the other person. We should guard our hearts so as not to take disagreements personally. We must take care to never regard losing a debate, even an important one, as "the end of the world."

This warning applies poignantly to the particular words we use. Kitchen adds, "How many arguments, rifts and fights could have been avoided by simply refraining from a single word!"[11] Avoid saying things such as, "in response to Bob," "this course of action is thoughtless or foolish," "this is unloving," "no one doubts the innocence of the accused," etc. Such responses are harsh in that they can come across as attacking people instead of arguments, they impute motives, and they bully those in opposition to your position.

But the mouth of fools pour out folly (v. 2b)

Kitchen's summary of this clause is apt: "The fool simply opens wide his mouth and lets flow whatever comes to his lips."[12] Instead of speaking because we can, we need to ask whether our speech is helpful and adds to the current discussion. I once witnessed a Presbytery "debate" in which there were roughly ten speeches in a row in favor of an action. The ensuing vote was unanimous. Remember that "When words are many, transgression is not lacking, but whoever restrains his lips is prudent" (Prov. 10:19).

Conversely, we can act foolishly in a debate due to lack of thoughtfulness and prayer before speaking. Kitchen says of the man in view here that "He speaks whatever comes to his mind and cares not for those who don't like it."[13] The intent of the speaker is not in view in this proverb as much as the attraction or repulsion that each kind of speech described brings. If we need to say things that are unattractive or unpopular, then let us at least aim to say them in an attractive way to the body before which we are speaking.

10   Ibid., 325.
11   Ibid.
12   Ibid., 326.
13   Ibid.

But perverseness in it breaks the spirit (v. 4b).

Perverseness involves twisted or crooked speech. This is possibly the worst abuse listed in these verses. It involves, "Twisting words so that they serve our own evil intent 'crushes the spirit' of those we are in relationship with."[14] This kind of speech aims to achieve our own ends without regarding explicitly Christ's glory or the edification of others. While we should never assume or imply that others are doing this during a debate, are any of us above temptation in this area?

For instance, if you have had a long-standing doctrinal or personal dispute with another presbyter who is brought under moral charges, could you not be tempted to use the occasion to try to "get rid of him"? I have seen men in such circumstances assume guilt before hearing the details of the case. This example also can go the other way. We can defend the actions of a presbyter due to an established friendship with him, blinding us to the evidence relevant to the debate at hand. We must show no partiality; neither must we be respecters of persons.

A Principle of Accountability

The eyes of the Lord are in every place (v. 3a)

The children's catechism teaches us, "I cannot see God, but he always sees me." The author of this proverb draws the implication from divine omniscience that if God sees all things, then He sees (or, hears) all that one says.[15] God knows all that we do and why we do it. He is more aware of us and of our motives than we are of ourselves. We must labor to speak with a good conscience before God and men (Acts 24:16).

Keeping watch over the evil and the good (v. 3b)

God examines the speech of all kinds of people. God's knowledge is a terror to the evil and a comfort to the good.[16] God's knowledge of

14   Ibid.
15   Ibid., 326.
16   Ibid.

all things should alarm the evil and bring the good to repentance and obedience. Paul applied this idea to the evil when he said, "The times of ignorance God overlooked, but now he commands all men everywhere to repent, because he has fixed a day on which he will judge the world in righteousness by a man whom he has appointed; and of this he has given assurance to all by raising him from the dead" (Acts 17:30-31). He applied it to the good, when he wrote, "For we must all appear before the judgment seat of Christ, so that each one may receive what is due for what he has done in the body, whether good or evil. Therefore, knowing the fear of the Lord, we persuade others" (2 Cor. 5:10-11a). No man is justified on the ground of his works before God (Rom. 3:20), but those who are justified must give an account of their service to God in Christ.

An awareness of God's knowledge of us should help us participate in church courts rather than paralyze us from participating in them.

We will never be entirely free of sinful speech on this side of glory, but we have potential to do much good with our speech when we speak in God's presence, through faith in Christ, with the Spirit's help.

When we consider speaking at Presbytery, we should ask ourselves several pointed questions: Am I speaking on the floor simply because I want my voice heard, or does my speech add to the substance of the debate at hand? Am I afraid to speak when others expect me to take their side in a debate and I disagree with them? Am I persuadable, listening to the arguments of others, or do I simply plan to vote as others expect me to? We should seek to do good through speaking in church courts, rather than simply enjoying the good privilege of speaking.

CONCLUDING DIRECTIONS FOR PRESBYTERS

Kitchen's conclusion to this section of Proverbs is a fitting summary of the content of this article. He wrote, "We are endowed by our Creator with the capacity to bring either genuine, substantive help to those around us or to inflict incalculable lasting harm upon them – all of that by simply opening our mouths!"[17] A few directions can help us apply further the teaching of Proverbs 15:1-4 in church courts.

1. Don't take things personally and don't make things personal. Speak to the moderator and leave previous speakers anonymous. Robert's Rules of Order requires this procedure for good reasons.

2. Beware of imputing motives to your brothers in debate. Assume the best of them rather than the worst.

3. Pray throughout debates, asking the Lord not only for what to say but how to say it well. It is alleged that during the Westminster Assembly debates over church government, George Gillespie, who was a heavy hitter in those debates, wrote repeatedly on his paper, "*da luce domine*," which means, "Lord give light." Whether this story is real or apocryphal, it is a useful reminder to pray at all times.

4. Remember that those with whom you disagree are not Scribes and Pharisees, but fellow presbyters and brothers in Christ. Love Christ by speaking the truth to them in love.

5. "Let your gentleness be evident to all, for the Lord is at hand" (Phil. 4:5).[18] Reformed Christians have not always cultivated the fruit of gentleness well, but our Lord did. Let us imitate His character by grace even as we long to see His face in glory. Let us be gentle in our speech.

Ryan McGraw (PhD, University of the Free State, Jonathan Edwards Centre Africa) is Professor of Systematic Theology at Greenville Presbyterian Theological Seminary. This chapter was adapted from a sermon delivered at the 83rd General Assembly of the Orthodox Presbyterian Church (OPC).

---

17   Ibid., 327.
18   επιεικες bears the connotation of yielding, gentleness, or kindness.

IN THESI DELIVERANCES

by C. N. Willborn

INTRODUCTION

American Presbyterianism has a number of ecclesiological issues which have garnered perennial attention. These include the minister/ elder and his adoption of the doctrinal standards of the church, the relationship of ruling and teaching elders within the polity of the church, the power of the courts, and, intimately related to the latter issue, the authority of *in thesi* deliverances of the highest judicatory of the church. The subject of this essay is that of *in thesi* deliverances and their authority to bind the consciences of men in the lower courts of the Presbyterian Church and their utility in shaping judicial cases in a lower court. Another way of posing the topic is this: Are *in thesi* deliverances of the General Assembly only "didactic, advisory, and monitory"?

Before entering into our discussion, we should first explain what the term *in thesi* means as used above and throughout this paper. It is a phrase used to refer to an answer given to a particular inquiry although the particular inquiry may concern that which is abstract or general in nature. So, a presbytery or session[1] brings a matter before the General Assembly desiring the highest judicatory of the church to render an opinion concerning their query; the General Assembly responds with an *in thesi* declaration. They have not rendered a judicial decision, for there was no judicial case before them. The General Assembly has simply given a good faith response to the request of a

---

[1] While the session of a local church would normally bring an overture through the presbytery to gain presbytery support and then the overture would be sent to the General Assembly by the presbytery, there are occasions when the presbytery does not endorse a session's overture and the session, feeling strongly about the issue, submits the overture directly to the General Assembly for consideration.

lower court, believing themselves to have correctly represented the teaching or intent of their constitution and, by inference, the only rule of faith and practice for a Presbyterian church, the Holy Bible.

The question most certainly follows as to whether the highest court's response to a *non-judicial* case can be said to bind the consciences of men or be used by the lower courts to construct judicial cases in the future? In other words, when the highest court speaks *in thesi*, does it speak with authority; is any one bound by its voice? From American Presbyterian history we wish to explore this question.

HISTORICAL PERSPECTIVE

The Westminster Confession of Faith addresses the ministerial and declarative power of synods and councils:

> It belongeth to synods and councils, ministerially to determine controversies of faith, and cases of conscience; to set down rules and directions for the better ordering of the public worship of God, and government of His Church; to receive complaints in cases of maladministration, and authoritatively to determine the same: which decrees and determinations, if consonant to the Word of God, are to be received with reverence and submission; not only for their agreement with the Word, but also for the power whereby they are made, as being an ordinance of God appointed thereunto in His Word. [2]

The Confession apparently recognizes three categories to which ecclesiastical office bearers speak ministerially: first, doctrinal and ethical controversies; second, the establishment and ordering of public worship and the government of the Church; and, third, appellate cases brought before a higher court.

William Cunningham, the outstanding Scottish theologian and churchman, sheds light on the meaning of the Confession, which serves to assist our view of court deliverances:

2 Westminster Confession of Faith 31.3. The edition used is that adopted by the Presbyterian Church in America and the Orthodox Presbyterian Church. In the section of chapter 31 no difference is found with the original Confession as adopted by the Church of Scotland in 1647.

Now this statement of the powers and functions of Church courts includes the whole subject of discipline and censures, though it comprehends also a great deal more, and the principles which directly or by plain implication it lays down in regard to *all* the judgments and decisions of ecclesiastical office-bearers are these: First, That unless they are consonant with the word of God, they are of no force or validity whatever ... and are entitled to no reverence or submission whatever from men; .... secondly, That such judgments and decisions, when professedly regulated by the word of God, and pronounced by competent parties,—that is, by ecclesiastical office-bearers,—are entitled to a careful and respectful examination; and, thirdly, That when accordant with the word of God, men, in dealing with and submitting to them, and in their whole views and feelings with respect to them, ought to be influenced not only by a regard to their actual accordance with the word ... but also, in addition, by a recognition of God's arrangement in establishing the ordinance of church government, and of its right and efficient working as a divine ordinance in the particular cases under consideration.[3]

Here it appears that Cunningham gives the General Assembly power to speak authoritatively not only to "discipline and censures" but "a great deal more," which he further iterates when he says the power of the court includes "the principles which directly or by plain implication it lays down in regard to *all* the judgments and decisions of ecclesiastical office-bearers." The principles to which he refers are laid out above as: faithfulness to God's word, declared by church officers, and the recognition on the receptor's part of the authority of God's ordinance of church government.

Cunningham's position is consistent with that of Robert Shaw in his commentary on the Confession. He explains that Confession 31.3 "is evidently intended as a decision upon another important principle in the controversy with Independents." The Independents admitted that a congregation might consult with a synod of ministers and find great advantage for themselves. However, Independents denied to these synods authority over the congregation. The position of the

3   William Cunningham, *Discussions on Church Principles* (1863; reprint, Edmonton, Canada: Still Waters Revival Books, 1991) 246.

Confession of Faith then, according to Shaw, was that Christ alone is the lawgiver of the church and the church "is only to apply and enforce the laws which he [Christ] has enacted." So, the power and function of the officers of the church is ministerial and declarative. Shaw points out that the declarations of the ecclesiastical office bearer "are to be considered, not as merely consultative [as the Independents avow], but authoritative." Furthermore, so far as the declarations of courts agree with the Holy Scriptures, "they must be binding upon the conscience."[4]

In the end, Cunningham, Shaw, and the 1880 Presbyterian Church in the United States (PCUS) are clear in saying that judicial renderings and *in thesi* deliverances of the General Assembly "not only deserve high consideration, but both must be submitted to, unless contrary to the Constitution and the Word." Therefore, the difference between the two is not found in the authoritative *nature* since both declarations of the church are ministerial and declarative; declarative of the law of the church, the Holy Scriptures. The church should speak to every matter before it according to Scripture or it should remain silent.

The Presbyterian Church in America (PCA), as the ecclesiastical successor to the PCUS, has engaged this question on several occasions. Indeed, the PCA has experienced the same problem as its predecessor—the lower courts' failure to take seriously Assembly deliverances—which led the PCA to add the following paragraph to her Constitution:

> Actions of the General Assembly pursuant to the provision of BCO 14-6 such as deliverances, resolutions, overtures, and judicial decisions are to be given due and serious consideration by the Church and its lower courts when deliberating matters related to such action. Judicial decisions shall be binding and conclusive on the parties who are directly involved in the matter being adjudicated, and may be appealed to in subsequent similar cases as to any principle which may have been decided. (See BCO 3-5 and 6,

4 Robert Shaw, *The Reformed Faith: An Exposition of the Confession of Faith of the Westminster Assembly* ... (1845; reprint, Inverness, Scotland: Christian Focus Publications, 1973) 312.

and *WCF* 31:3)[5]

According to this constitutional provision, all sorts of deliverances are "to be given due and serious consideration by the Church and its lower courts when deliberating matters related to such action." While deliverances are not to be taken lightly and are to be considered by lower courts when considering similar cases, there is no authoritative or binding nature attributed to them. Judicial decisions, on the other hand, are "binding and conclusive on the parties ... directly involved ... and may be appealed to in subsequent similar cases." Thus, the PCA makes the general response of the General Assembly to overtures of *some* authority, enough that they demand "due and serious consideration." To judicial decisions, the PCA makes the specific application of Church law to a specific case of *absolute* authority, so that they are "binding and conclusive."

Conclusion

The concerns godly men have had for the Presbyterian Church to act like deliberate and biblically conscious churchmen is still a concern. As the nascent PCA felt its way through issues like the extraordinary gifts of the apostles, the novelty of pædo-communion, and confessional subscription, she has often left the impression that her unity hinges upon diversity and that she cannot speak definitively and univocally. Some have wondered just how many confessions of faith actually exist within the church. Yet, we declare to and publish for the world one Confession of Faith. Which is it—The Confession as approved by the General Assembly or the one approved by *this* presbytery or *that* presbytery? May pædo-communionists preach, teach, and practice their novel, contra-confessional views in her churches? What of extraordinary gifts in the church? Is a pastoral letter, issued *in thesi* by a General Assembly authoritative and binding so as to permit multiple, and often contradictory views, to exists in a denomination? What does that say about a church's view of Scripture and its perspicacity and authority?

Similarly, the Assembly annually meets for business and deliberates

5 Presbyterian Church in America, *Book of Church Order* (Lawrenceville, GA: The Committee for Christian Education and Publications) 14-7.

matters of significance to a variety of presbyteries as they come by way of overtures. The Assembly declares itself on the various issues and what happens? Presbyteries walk away thinking the particular deliverance was for someone else, but does not bind them to do anything differently than before.

From all we have seen above, there is no basis historically or constitutionally for *in thesi* deliverances to be taken lightly. They should have an effect on the way every presbytery thinks about and goes about her business. From the 1880 decision of the PCUS General Assembly, to Scottish fathers like William Cunningham and Robert Shaw, we have heard the wise words of the Fathers — "Listen carefully to the collective wisdom of the church." If Presbyterianism means anything, it means that no church is an island; we are a part of the whole. One contemporary PCA churchman explains the relevance of *in thesi* deliverances in the following manner:

> In actuality, the GA makes such statements to advise its members and churches of the mind of the larger church at that moment. While such action does not have the authority of law to bind conscience or future Assemblies, brothers in Christ are obligated to weigh with great deference this "pious advice" since they have vowed to seek the peace and purity of the church, and this cannot be done through simply ignoring the properly approved advice of brothers and fathers.[6]

As one can see from this statement, there is great reason for an *in thesi* deliverance of the General Assembly to obligate every presbyter and presbytery to consider and apply the "pious advice" of the gathered Assembly of divines. Why should *in thesi* deliverances not be considered "pious" and be taken seriously? After all, the ecclesiastical office-bearers of the church have issued a deliverance they believe to be consistent with their constitutional documents.

Nevertheless, we do admit there is a difference between the constitu-

---

6 Bryan Chapell, former President of Covenant Seminary, made these comments in response to the Presbyterian and Reformed Joint Commission on Chaplains and Military Personnel. They appear in Note 1 of "PRJC Letter Regarding Women in Combat" available through the PCA Office of Administration.

tional law of the church, the judicial decisions of the supreme judicatory, and *in thesi* deliverances.

The difference between judicial renderings and *in thesi* deliverances, it would seem, have to do with the manner in which each stand to the church. *In thesi* deliverances stand as a provisional response to a general concern of the church (albeit the concern may be as specific as what a confessional phrase means, e.g., "the space of six days"). They are a provisional response, yet consistent with our constitution according to human wisdom. In contrast to the Assembly's issuance of an *in thesi* deliverance, a judicial decision stands as a final redress of a specific matter. In other words, when an overture comes before the General Assembly and the Assembly responds, she does not respond in her relation to the lower courts as the "last resort." It is only when the Assembly decides a specific case—as the case has been brought to her through proper process—as she settles the constitutional right or wrong of a specific case, that she speaks as the court of "last resort." When the General Assembly speaks as the court of "last resort," she speaks with her ultimate authoritative voice. In the context of the "last resort," the church is saying "thus saith the Lord." Appeal can be taken no higher.

The question remains, however, are *in thesi* deliverances of the General Assembly authoritative? Yes, because the court is presumed to have spoken consistent with her constitution. Are they the final word on a given subject? No, because they are not specific to a case. Should they simply be dismissed as "non-binding" and, thus, superfluous? No, because they reflect the wisdom of the church. Should they be allowed simply to collect archival dust? No, because ideas have consequences. If they are important and profitable, they should receive further church-wide consideration and perhaps further explanation, and expounding so as to become the proposition of the church formally. If they are dangerous to the long-term health of the church, they should be exposed, and consequently expunged from the records of the church so as to remove the likelihood of confusion and future conflict.

When a court of the church hands down a "didactic, advisory, and monitory" deliverance, it behooves elders to act as churchmen for the good of the whole, not Independents concerned only with their local church. Men need to begin to think presbytery-wide, and assembly-wide; thinking for the good of the whole, not just the part. The latter really is the only way to offset the all-too-present lackadaisical approach to *in thesi* deliverances and the "Independent tendency" in American Presbyterianism.

C.N. Willborn (PhD, Westminster Theological Seminary) is Adjunct Professor of Church History at Greenville Presbyterian Theological Seminary. This chapter was adapted from his "The "Ministerial and Declarative" Powers of the Church and In Thesi Deliverances," in The Confessional Presbyterian, *2005, 94-101. Used by permission.*

CONFESSIONAL SUBSCRIPTION

by Morton H. Smith

A creedal or confessional statement is a statement of what an individual or a denomination confesses to be his or its belief. That creedal statements are Biblical is seen in the faithful sayings that the Apostle cites in the Pastoral Epistles. For example, "This is a faithful saying and worthy of all acceptation, That Christ Jesus came into the world to save sinners, of whom I am chief" (1 Tim. 1:15). The PCA, as it came into being, declared herself to be committed to the Westminster Confession and Catechisms as held by the American Presbyterian Churches since 1789.

The idea of subscription is that of formal committing of oneself to that to which he subscribes. The second ordination vow of the PCA is a vow in which the ordinand affirms his faith. It involves his subscription to the Westminster Confession and Catechisms as the confession of his faith. It reads:

> Do you sincerely receive and adopt the Confession of Faith and the Catechisms of this Church, as containing the system of doctrine taught in the Holy Scriptures; and do you further promise that if at any time you find yourself out of accord with any of the fundamentals of this system of doctrine, you will on your own initiative, make known to your Presbytery (Session) the change which has taken place in your views since the assumption of this ordination vow? (BCO 21-5, 24-5)

Before going further, it would be well to define what we understand the terms "strict" and "loose" subscription to mean. First, the two words "strict" and "loose" are not the best terms by which to describe the two views at play in the "subscription debate." This terminology goes back to the nineteenth century. In some ways, both terms are caricatures of the positions bearing these names. Instead of "strict subscription," the better description is "full subscription." For the expression "loose subscription," we may substitute "system of theology subscription," which shall be abbreviated as "system subscription" throughout this paper.

Strict or full subscription takes at face value the question above, "Do you sincerely receive and adopt the Confession of Faith and the Catechisms of this Church, as containing the system of doctrine taught in the Holy Scriptures..." It holds that the ordinand is subscribing to nothing more or less than the entirety of the Confession and Catechisms as containing the system of doctrine taught in the Scriptures. This is not to say that the full subscriptionist does not recognize the some of the teachings of the Confession and Catechisms are more foundational than others, but it is to say that the full subscriptionist believes that in professing that the Confession and Catechisms of this Church are his confession, that he is subscribing to all of the doctrines in the Confession and Catechisms. They are all part of the system of doctrine, though admittedly some are more essential than others. Note that full subscription does not require subscription in terms of adopting every word of the Confession and Catechisms, but rather in terms of every doctrine or teaching of the Confession and Catechisms.

Loose – or system – subscription, on the other hand, maintains that we subscribe to a system of doctrine which is not specifically defined, but which is contained in the Confession and Catechisms of the Church. System subscription holds to the adoption of all the fundamental and essential doctrines of the system. Other expressions of the Confessions and Catechisms, which are not judged to be essential to the system of doctrine are a matter of indifference, whether the ordinand adopts them or not.

Involved in both of these views is the concept of "doctrine." Essentially the word means a teaching. When the full subscriptionist insists on the fact that our subscription includes all of the doctrines in the Confessional Standards, he is not insisting on every statement regarding each of these doctrines, but rather that each of the areas of teaching dealt with by the Standards is included in his subscription. The system subscriptionist maintains, on the other hand, that only the doctrines comprising the system are mandated in the subscription. Those propositions or expressions, and even those doctrines that are not a part of the system are not included. The definition of what is included in the system is one that is to be determined by the courts of the Church as the occasion arises.

Let us illustrate the kinds of differences that arise. The full subscriptionist believes that he is committed to every doctrinal position set forth in the Confession and Catechisms. He is thus committed to the view of marriage and divorce set forth in the Confession. If a member of his church desires to marry a Roman Catholic, which is specifically spoken against in the Confession, the full subscriptionist would not feel that he has the liberty to perform such a marriage, but rather must warn his parishioner against such a marriage. The system subscriptionist may view that part of the chapter on marriage as not a part of the system, and might feel that he would be at perfect liberty to perform such a marriage.

A number of other illustrations could be presented, such as, views of the Sabbath, of the conduct of worship services, etc. The full subscriptionist holds to the Sabbath as set forth in the Catechisms, while the system subscriptionist may feel that he is at liberty to do a number of things forbidden by the Catechisms. Such is the case with the regulative principle of worship. The full subscriptionist views this as the position of the Presbyterian Church, and does not want crosses or pictures of Christ, in the place of worship. He also wants to be able to point directly to Scripture for everything he does do in his worship service. The system subscriptionist may feel that the use of crosses, or even of pictures of Christ, is permissible. He judges this part of the Catechism as one to which exception may be taken, since he may not feel that the Scriptural system of doctrine requires it. When we see how our views of subscription apply to our public practice, we see why there can be such a tension between the two groups.

The question must be answered as to how the exceptions are to be treated. We shall now seek to set forth the implications of each of the viewpoints as we see them.

First, one could hold that no exceptions should be allowed. When one subscribes to the Confession of a church, he adopts that confession as his own, and will not teach or practice that which is contrary to this confession. He determines, by the help of God, that he will seek to be true to the Faith both in his teaching and in his life. This is the position that the full subscriptionist prefers. It is not, however, the only position compatible to the full subscriptionist position.

Provision was made from the first Adopting Act (1729) of the American Presbyterian Church for men to state their scruples to the examining Presbytery. The Presbytery then had the duty of determining whether the point of the exception is of such a nature as to exclude the candidate from the Presbyterian ministry or not. For those allowed to be ordained with exceptions, the question remains as to what this allowance permits. Is he permitted to teach his view, which is not in accord with the Standards of the Church, or is he required to teach the position of the Church?

The full subscriptionist maintains that the allowance of the exception is not an agreement for the individual to teach against the doctrines of the Church. If the candidate desires to be a Presbyterian minister, he must be willing to submit himself to the brethren, and teach only what the Church has adopted as its position. If he cannot do this in good conscience, then he should seek a fellowship where he is not under such a stricture. Samuel Miller (1769-1850) wrote regarding this question:

> Set it down, then, as a first principle of common honesty, as well as of Christian truth, that subscription to Articles of Faith, is a weighty transaction, which really means what it professes to mean; that no man is ever at liberty to subscribe articles which he does not truly and fully believe; and that, in subscribing, he brings himself under a solemn, covenant engagement to the church which he enters, to walk with it 'in the unity of faith,' and 'in the bond of

peace and love.' If he cannot do this honestly, let him not profess to do it at all.[1]

The ordinand who takes exceptions to a particular teaching of the Confession or Catechisms, may be ordained by the Presbytery, if it feels that the exception does not impinge upon the basic system of doctrine contained in the Standards. He is not thereby permitted to teach contrary to the Standards. He should teach the view of the Standards, so as not to disturb the Church by teaching contrary to her Standards. If one is not able thus to subject himself to the brethren, he should seek some other communion, where he has greater liberty.

The Confession and Catechisms of the Church are its creed, not some undefined system of doctrine – not even an undefined Reformed system of doctrine. Theological liberals in the Mainline Presbyterian Church of the early twentieth century, all of whom were loose subscriptionists, claimed to hold to the system of doctrine, but not to the Confession and Catechisms themselves. By not defining the system, they were able to affirm this, and not be brought under discipline, when they taught something contrary to the Confession or Catechisms. If we permit men to take exceptions to the Confession and Catechisms, and then allow them to teach their exceptions, the Church will become less and less unified on its doctrinal position. It will become increasingly more and more difficult to discipline those who teach error. The Church in its creed has declared what it believes is the proper interpretation of the various doctrines contained therein. This is the view that the Church expects her minister to teach and uphold. If a man desires to be a minister in a confessional denomination, he must be willing to submit his personal teaching and practices to the Church, even though he feels that the Church is not correct at the particular point in question. If he cannot do so, then he should seek another fellowship.

The writers of the Confession and Catechisms were very wise in not settling all possible theological questions on which the Bible is not explicit. For example, the Standards do not settle the matters of su-

1 Samuel Miller, *The Utility and Importance of Creeds and Confessions: addressed particularly to candidates for the ministry* (Greenville, SC: 1987), 102.

pra- or infralapsarianism, or of the nature of the imputation of Adam's sin, or of millennialism. Happily, the Westminster divines left these as matters for the individual conscience, and we are not bound by a particular view on them by our subscription to the Standards.

The spirit of our subscription is one of submission to the brethren, but even more it is one of submission to the Word of God. This has historically been the spirit expressed in the Reformed and Presbyterian confessions. The Scots Confession of 1560 declares in its preface:

> If any man will note in our Confession any chapter or sentence contrary to God's Holy Word, that it would please him of his gentleness and for Christian charity's sake to inform us of it in writing; and we, upon our honour, do promise him that by God's grace we shall give him satisfaction from the mouth of God, that is, from Holy Scripture, or else shall alter whatever he can prove to be wrong.

In closing, it is incumbent on us to learn the lessons of history, and to seek to resolve this problem that has caused no shortage of disturbance of the "peace and purity" of the American Presbyterian Church.

Morton H. Smith (PhD, Free University of Amsterdam) is Professor Emeritus of Systematic Theology at Greenville Presbyterian Theological Seminary. This chapter was adapted from his The Subscription Debate: Studies in Presbyterian Polity, *pages 16-41.*

THE DIACONATE
by George W. Knight III

The word Deacon, which designates a specific office in the church, translates the Greek word διακονος. Διακονος has been rendered in English by deacon in Phil. 1:1 and 1 Tim. 3:6 and 12 where the translators thought that the context indicated that this special office was in view. In doing so they were using one of the specialized senses of the Greek word διακονος which means in its most basic sense "servant" (cf. for example Mt. 22:11; John 2:5, 9). Thus the word is used of all Christians of their relationship to the Lord and to one another (cf. Mt. 20:25-28, Mk. 10:42-45; John 12:26). And it is also used of those serving the church as leaders, and in those cases the English translation is often that of "minister," indicating a slightly more restricted sense of the Greek word διακονος (cf. Eph. 6:21; Col. 4:7; 1 Tim. 4:6). These church officers, or leaders, are designated by other terms, such as elders, overseers, pastors, and teachers. But those officers whose role is so characteristic of service are always in the New Testament designated only by the term deacon (servant), using διακονος in this specialized sense of a particular church officer.

That designation of servant links these officers with their great example and model, Jesus Christ the Servant of the Lord. He points to his own life of service as the model for Christians when he says in Mark 10:43-45: "whoever wants to become great among you must be your servant, and whoever wants to be first must be slave of all. For the Son of Man did not come to be served, but to serve..." One of the ways that Jesus served was in feeding the multitudes and in caring for the needy. He showed particular compassion for widows and welcomed little ones to himself and blessed them. In this activity he fulfilled that which James summarizes as the essence of pure religion: "Religion that God our Father accepts as pure and faultless is this: to look after orphans and widows in their distress..." (James 1:27). He is the model for all Christians and particularly for Deacons.

Deacons are mentioned in Paul's letter to the Philippians and in his first letter to Timothy as recognized officers in the church. But where and how does the office of the deacon first manifest itself in the New Testament? The answer to that question is to be found in the Apostolic action of instituting a separate group of men to assist them and have special responsibilities. We read about that decision and its outcome in Acts 6 where the Apostles indicate to the disciples that they should choose seven men from among themselves for a particular responsibility.

The warrant for seeing those seven men in Acts 6 as the first deacons is evidenced by the following considerations. First, even though the word "deacon" (διακονος) is not used in the passage to designate these seven men, their task, "to serve [wait on] tables" (Acts 6:2), is related in the Greek text by διακονειν, the verb cognate to the noun "deacon" (διακονος). And this relationship is not only one of language but also of task. The task of serving tables is certainly appropriate for those who will be later called servants or deacons. Second, the particular responsibilities of apostles and the seven men indicated in Acts 6 is virtually identical to the particular responsibilities of elders (or overseers) and deacons stated in other passages in the New Testament. And just as apostles have alongside of them the seven men so also the elders (or overseers) have alongside of them the deacons (Phil. 1:1; 1 Tim. 3:1-13). The apostles speak of their own labors as that of the word and prayer (Acts 6:5), not to mention ruling, and the same function is that given to elders or bishops (overseers) (cf., e.g., Acts 20:28; 1 Tim. 3:2, 3; Titus 1:9). The seven men are called to serve in Acts 6:2 and 3 (διακονειν) and the same is said of the deacons in I Tim. 3:10 and 13(διακονειν). Third, the seven men are to be chosen from those who manifest certain spiritual qualifications (Acts 6:3). The Deacons are to be chosen from men who manifest similar spiritual qualifications (I Tim. 3:8-10 and 12). Although the two sets of qualifications are not identical, the more specific list in I Timothy 3 could easily be seen as the specifications of the more general outline of Acts 6. There is no obstacle to equating the seven men and the

Deacons and much to commend it.

The diaconal work in view in Acts 6 is initially carried on by the Apostles. They do so because of two reasons. First, the work committed to the people of God is often best, but not exclusively, carried on by the church through its officers or representatives. Second, it would appear that the Apostles include within their function and office the regular functions and offices of the church, namely that of elder and deacon. By analogy, it may be correctly presumed that the office of elder also includes the functions and office of deacon. This may be the reason why only elders are elected in the new churches mentioned in Acts 14:23 and in Titus 1:5ff.

The Apostles, however, in Acts 6 determine that they can no longer adequately handle the diaconal function and particularly that they cannot do so without forsaking that function which is their prime responsibility, i.e., the Word of God (Acts 6:2). Thus the office of the first deacons, the seven men, comes into existence to continue to meet the specific physical needs of the widows, especially their need for food (Acts 6:1 and 2), and also at the same time to help the apostles and relieve them of "this task" (Acts 6:3 NASB, "this responsibility" NIV). These seven men in their ministry of serving tables do so as men "of good reputation, full of the Spirit and of wisdom" (Acts 6:3 NASB). This account serves as a model for determining the ministry of deacons since nowhere else in the Scriptures are their tasks specified. This model shows them performing a spiritual ministry to those within the church who need the basic necessities of life provided for them. This is the first and main principle with which this account provides us. The second and related principle is that of providing assistance to those who rule and teach in the church and carrying out those "tasks" or "responsibilities" which must be accomplished by the officers of the church and which the elders cannot do without detriment to their main function as the spiritual pastors of the people of God. But these other tasks which they may appropriately be assigned must not cause the deacons themselves to forsake the specific task of deacons, namely, the ministry of mercy to those in need.

That the deacons work in subjection to the elders and their rule, even in the area of finances and, specifically, the funds for the needy, is not only evident from the fact that the elders are required to rule over the entire church and all its organizations and officers, including the deacons, but also is demonstrated by the particular passage of Acts 11:27-30. The famine relief funds sent to Jerusalem are given over to the elders (verse 30). The elders, like the apostles, are to be concerned for the victims of the famine and oversee and provide for them. Thus the funds come to the elders. But like the apostles, even though it is not stated in the text and does not need to be stated in the light of Acts 6, we may presume that the elders committed this business to the deacons to accomplish the actual distribution.

It might be argued from the further activity of Stephen and Philip (Acts 8:5ff.), who are listed among the seven men of Acts 6 (verse 5), that their activity indicates that deacons should also be evangelists, i.e., preachers. Certainly Philip in Acts 8 is an evangelist and is engaged in preaching in a very full sense of the word. However, it is not as one of the seven men whose job it is to serve tables for the widows in Jerusalem that he is engaged in these activities away from Jerusalem. This distinction and evaluation is borne out by the text of Acts 21:8 where Philip's ministry as an evangelist is distinguished from his being, or having been, one of the seven men: "...Philip the evangelist, one of the Seven." This is also borne out by the description of the activities specifically given to the seven men in Acts 6. They were to "serve tables" and assist the widows and engage in similar activities in order to relieve the Apostles so that they could preach and minister the Word. The description of the task of the seven men in Acts 6 — especially when seen in the light of what the Apostles were to do in contrast with them — defines the diaconal work of the seven men and the deacons and does not include what Philip later does. His activity later is his work as an evangelist not as one of the seven men, and these two activities in which Philip was engaged one after the other must not be confused with one another.

This distinction is also borne out by a comparison of the lists of qualifications for overseers and deacons in 1 Tim. 3:1-13. It is said of overseers (elders) that they must be "able to teach" (verse 2, cf. Titus 1:9 and also the further distinction among elders in 1 Tim. 5:17) and that they must take care of God's church (verse 5), neither of these two things is said of deacons in 1 Tim. 3:8-13, even though the deacons and elders have other qualifications that are common or similar.

Certain distinctive qualifications of deacons indicated in 1 Tim. 3:8-13 may well help to underscore the sensitive and important interpersonal relationships which deacons will be involved in while ministering to the needy. They would not of themselves establish the area of labor, as Acts 6 does explicitly, but on the background of that passage their meaning and significance are more readily recognized.

The reference to women or wives in 1 Tim. 3:11 is set in the midst of a passage which describes those to whom the designation deacon (διακονος) is applied as men (cf. verses 8 and 12, the latter in which the deacon is said to be the husband). Who are these females referred to in verse 11? Several answers have been given, but because of the brevity of the paper I will restrict these comments to the answer I consider most in harmony with the biblical context here and elsewhere.[1] The Greek word γυνη (in the plural) which is rendered "wives" by the NIV, and which is rendered by other translations as "women", can mean either depending upon the context. Its use in the very close context of both verses 2 and 12 with the meaning wife favors the meaning wife here. This rendering also explains other aspects of verse 11. If indeed the wife is in view, as I believe she is, this would explain the location of the verse in the middle of the discussion of the deacon and right before the statement about his marital and family qualifications. This statement about his wife is then the first of those familial statements and therefore it is not an intrusion. Furthermore, reference to his wife can best explain the absence of reference to marital fidelity for the wife which is otherwise always present (cf. 1 Tim. 3:2,12 and 5:9). The Greek transitional word ωσαυτως — rendered in the NIV with the phrase "in the same way" — both distinguishes and correlates this verse and the one in it from and with the deacon. The distinguishing aspect shows that she is not a deacon or deaconess, and the correlating aspect shows that she is one who has similar qualifications and thus is qualified to assist her husband. The church today should give heed to both aspects of

1 For a fuller discussion, see Dr. Knight's *The Pastoral Epistles* (NIGTC).

this verse and act accordingly. In the light of this passage and in the light of the fact that the Apostles specifically required the church to elect "men" in Acts 6:3 (as they did, Acts 6:5; the Greek word ανηρ used in Acts 6:3 designates a "male" and is different from the Greek word ανθρωπος that means a human being), it is best to understand the usage of διακονος with reference to Phoebe in Romans 16:1 to be used in the same general sense of servant as it is used in the only other reference in Romans (13:4ff.) and not as a designation of her as a deacon or deaconess (this general sense of servant is found in a number of modern translations). 1 Timothy 3 applies the title deacon to a male officer (verses 2 and 12). The consistency between Acts 6 and 1 Timothy 3 provides the biblical basis for deacons being men.

What consolation and encouragement is there for deacons in performing such tasks of service to the needy and such assistance to the elders? Many could be mentioned but let one suffice, that of the Apostle Paul himself in 1 Tim. 3:13: "Those who have served well gain an excellent standing and great assurance in their faith in Christ Jesus."

George W. Knight III (PhD, Free University of Amsterdam) is Professor Emeritus of New Testament at Greenville Presbyterian Theological Seminary. He is a former President of the Evangelical Theological Society. This chapter was reprinted from his "The Biblical Foundation of the Diaconate," in Ordained Servant vol. 5, no. 3 (July 1996). Used by Permission.

LEADING IN WORSHIP
by Joseph A. Pipa, Jr.

Because of the corporate nature of public worship, its leadership is to be representative, namely, one person acts on behalf of all. Many aspects of worship, like singing and reading or reciting the confessions, are done by all. Other times, when the leader prays, he forms words for all. Who, then, is authorized to represent the congregation in corporate worship?

ROLES IN WORSHIP — I TIMOTHY 2:8-15

One of the most serious crises facing the church today is the role of men and women in the life of the congregation. On the one hand, there are those who believe that women should have the right to read Scripture or lead in prayer in public worship—some even asserting that women should have the right to deliver exhortations in the public assembly—while, on the other hand, there are those who say that only the minister should lead in worship. In 1 Timothy 2:8-15, Paul gives clear instruction on this matter, as he discusses the role of men and women in corporate worship.

THE ROLE OF MEN IN CORPORATE WORSHIP

The Requirement for Male Leadership (v. 8)

In verse 8, the apostle addresses the role of men in corporate worship: "Therefore I want the men in every place to pray, lifting up holy hands, without wrath and dissension." We rightly infer from verse 1 of 1 Timothy 2 that the term prayer may refer to the work of the church in corporate worship. The context enforces this interpretation. In verses 1-7, he addresses the church with respect to her concern for the world. This concern will be expressed in corporate prayer. In verses 9-11, he deals with women, primarily in the context of corporate worship. Compare his command in verse 11 with 1 Corinthians 14:33, 34.

Moreover, his use of the phrase "every place" would suggest that he means in all the places where the church assembles for worship; when the church meets to offer prayers of entreaty, supplication, thanksgiving, praise, and adoration in corporate worship (see 1 Corinthians 4:17; 11:16; 14:33.).

He begins with an apostolic injunction, "I want." This construction—that is, the verb *want* or *will* followed by an infinitive (in this case, the verb *to pray*) — is used in Scripture to indicate an apostolic commandment. (see 1 Timothy 5:14; Philippians 1:12.) Therefore, in every place where the church gathers for worship, the men are to lead.

Is it, however, the work of all men? By implication, the answer is no. It is the work of a special group of men. First, they must be approved men. Otherwise, how else will it be determined whether they possess the character mentioned at the end of the verse: "lifting up holy hands, without wrath and dissension"?

By the first term "holy," Paul refers to the character of the one who leads in worship. He uses hands as a figure of speech for character. Our hands often are the agents of good or evil. Therefore, the Bible uses hands to describe holiness. For example, the psalmist answers the question — "Who may ascend into the hill of the LORD? And who may stand in His Holy Place?"— with the description— "He who has clean hands and a pure heart, who has not lifted up his soul to falsehood, and has not sworn deceitfully" (Psalm 24:3, 4; cf. 26:6). The part is representative of the whole. Hence, the holy hands lifted in prayer is a figure of speech used to indicate the requirement that the man who leads the people of God in worship must be a man who is characterized by holiness. The psalmist emphasizes the importance of this injunction in Psalm 66:18: "If I regard wickedness in my heart, The Lord will not hear." Therefore, if the ungodly are offering prayers on behalf of the congregation, their worship will be hindered.

Paul mentions two things pastorally about the man who leads in worship: he is to be "without wrath and dissension." He must be a gentle man. The term "wrath" refers to unbridled anger. The man who leads must be gentle – a tender shepherd who bears long with the congregation.

The word translated "dissension" may mean either doubting or disputatious, and both would be very appropriate here. James instructs us that we are not to pray doubting, wavering in unbelief (1:6). Paul, however, uses the term to mean disputatious, one who is always arguing. Perhaps he has in mind the false teachers (1:6; 6:4). There must be a bond of sympathy between the congregation and the one who leads them in worship. He cannot be a wrathful or a disputatious man, because there will be those in the congregation whom he has alienated by his pugnacious spirit. If he is quick to wrath, he will create a barrier between those for whom he speaks and himself. If he is constantly disputing, he loses the confidence of those whom he leads.

Again, this requirement reminds us why the one who leads in worship is to be ordained or, at least, approved by the session or presbytery. He must be a holy man. Paul will expand on the character of church leaders in the next chapter, but, obviously, the one who leads in worship must be examined with respect to his character. (See 1 Timothy 3:1-7; Titus 1:5-9.)

Second, Paul implies that to lead in prayer is an act of authority. We infer the necessity of authority from Paul's prohibition of women exercising authority in the church (2:12). Corporate worship, by its very nature, suggests authority. One is to frame prayers for the people of God in the special presence of God; therefore, the one who frames prayers for the congregation exercises authority. Because he prays for all, he must have theological discernment; he must be grounded in Scripture. William Perkins says that the responsibility to lead the congregation in prayer is part of the office of the minister. As a prophet speaks to the people on behalf of God, so he speaks to God on behalf of the people.

A third ground for this interpretation is the matter of gifts. Not all men have the gift of speaking in an edifying manner in public. Those with this gift are to be the ones that lead in public prayer. Hence, the prayers for the congregation are to be offered by one set aside for that task.

By further inference, Paul includes all aspects of the worship service which involve leadership. First, the term "prayer" is used for the corporate worship of the church. Hence, to lead in prayer is to lead in worship; all actions of leadership in worship are to be performed by men (prayer, reading of Scripture, leading in public confession of faith, etc.). Second, in verse 11, Paul instructs women to "quietly receive instruction with entire submissiveness." A third reason is that later Paul tells the minister through Timothy to read the Scriptures publicly and to preach (1 Timothy 4:13).

Historically, the church's position on this has been that one who is ordained or who is under trial for ordination should read the Word of God. "The reading of the Word is God's direct address to His people. As such, it should be performed by someone who is specifically a leader in the Church—that is, by someone who has been ordained to the gospel ministry (including elders), or who has been licensed to preach, or who is, at least, an eligible candidate for ministry. The reading of the Word in public worship is an aspect of the pastoral ministry which should not be done by just anyone, even as preaching should not be (see I Tim. 4:13ff)."

What about Paul's instruction in 1 Corinthians 11:5: "But every woman who has her head uncovered while praying or prophesying disgraces her head"? The reference to praying refers to participation in public worship. We will deal with the matter of prophesying in verse 11.

Therefore, the church should limit this role to ministers, elders, and those approved by the church in preparation for ministry. The Larger Catechism applies the same principle to the reading of Scripture: "Although all are not to be permitted to read the word publickly to the congregation" (WLC 156). The Westminster Directory for the Publick Worship of God says, "Reading of the word in the congregation, being part of the publick worship of God . . . is to be performed by the pastors and teachers. Howbeit, such as intend the ministry, may occasionally both read the word, and exercise their gift in preaching in the congregation, if allowed by the presbytery thereunto." Because ruling elders are ordained as pastors, they, too, have the authority to lead in prayer and read Scripture in the public assembly.

Paul, therefore, distinguishes between the role of men and women in public worship. Building on the Old Testament pattern of worship, public worship is to be led by men. It is an apostolic commandment.

WOMEN IN CORPORATE WORSHIP (VV. 9, 10)

The requirement for approved men to lead in worship is reinforced by Paul's discussion of the role of women. Paul mentions the role of men briefly, almost in a passing manner, but he concentrates on the role of women. With respect to male leadership in worship, he builds on the Old Testament, but he is constrained to deal in greater detail with women, since the New Testament emphasizes the equality of women in the congregation. Paul wants us to know that equality in Christ does not remove God's ordained structure of authority. Moreover, other difficulties that had been brought into the church by Gentile converts needed to be addressed, namely, the matter of apparel and modesty. Because of the great confusion on this issue in the church today, I will expand.

Her Character

In verses 9 and 10, the apostle addresses character, what I call female piety: "Likewise, I want women to adorn themselves with proper clothing, modestly and discreetly, not with braided hair and gold or pearls or costly garments, but rather by means of good works, as is proper for women making a claim to godliness." Paul begins with a comparison, "likewise" or "in like manner." He often uses this term to make a comparison or a contrast. He will use this term in chapter 3 to distinguish deacons from elders, and wives from deacons. The term "likewise" connects what he is about to state with the apostolic injunction "I want." "To adorn" is grammatically parallel to the word "to pray," both are governed by the word "I want." I want the men to pray, I want women to adorn themselves, and thus the contrast is very clear in the very structure of the text. With respect to men, he begins with their work and concludes with their character. With respect to women, he begins with their character and concludes with their work.

He begins by commanding women to dress appropriately: "adorn themselves with proper clothing." The word translated "adorn" refers to her appearance. The verb can also mean "to decorate." It is used in Revelation 21:2 to describe the church as the "bride adorned for her husband." The phrase "proper clothing" translates two terms. The term "clothing" literally means deportment and refers to behavior, particularly expressed in one's apparel. The apparel is to be that which is "proper," respectable, or honorable. The root word of "proper" is cosmos, that which is orderly. It is the word translated "respectable" in 1 Timothy 3:2. Paul says there is apparel that is more appropriate for worship. In this day of informality, we need to be reminded that we are dressing to come into the presence of the King. Public worship takes place in the special presence of God (1 Corinthians 11:10; Psalm 100:4).

Paul expands on the concept of appropriate clothing both positively and negatively. Positively, Paul says she is to dress "modestly and discreetly." The term "modest" means that which avoids shame and embarrassment. Paul instructs a woman to have a chaste demeanor that does not draw attention to herself in a wrong way. She is to avoid dressing or acting in a way that would bring shame and embarrassment. Is it not interesting that this was a problem in the first century, as it is today? A woman's dress should be modest always, but particularly in public worship. A woman's apparel ought not to draw attention to her body: short dresses, exposure of cleavage, bare backs, and exposed midriffs would all violate this principle. It is difficult to fathom why a father would let his daughter walk out of the house dressed in a way that draws attention to her body. I cannot understand a husband who lacks a proper sense of jealousy by allowing his wife to appear in public, let alone in the worshipping assembly, dressed immodestly. Yet, there is hardly a church that one can attend in which immodest dress is not a problem.

Paul joins "discreetly" with modesty. The term means with discernment or prudence (1 Timothy 3:2; Titus 2:2, 5). Solomon says in Proverbs 11:22, "As a ring of gold in a swine's snout, so is a beautiful woman who lacks discretion." This combination of modesty with discernment is interesting because some women are quite naïve and do not understand that how they dress affects men. They often tempt a man to sin by their dress, or, at least, distract his attention in public worship. Moreover, the term suggests that she is to adorn herself in good taste, with sound judgment and self-control, not chasing every fad of fashion, particularly those that are immodest.

Negatively, he addresses the matter of ostentatious and extravagant dress: "not with braided hair and gold or pearls or costly garments." The Bible is not at all opposed to a woman being well dressed and as attractive as she can be, as we know from other passages of Scripture (Genesis 24:47, 53; Proverbs 31:22). Paul, in fact, begins this section by speaking of her adorning herself. We know that God loves beauty. He has ornamented the entire world and there is nothing wrong with beauty. There is nothing wrong with female beauty as long as the woman is not seeking to draw attention to herself in such a way as to make her enticing in the eyes of men other than her husband. What Paul is warning against is ostentatious and extravagant dress. When he joins together braided hair with gold or pearls, he seems to be alluding to the custom of the wealthy, who would elaborately braid their hair with costly jewels, gold, and pearls as a way of proclaiming their wealth. When joined with extravagant clothing, it was ostentatious. Paul is not forbidding dressing in style or having quality clothing, but dressing in a way that unduly draws attention to oneself and one's wealth. Particularly in public worship, one ought not to dress in a way that makes a poor person ashamed of his or her best dress.

Before we leave this section, it is important to note that we might have a biblical principle to aid in interpreting Paul in 1 Corinthians 11:1-15 on head covering. Is Paul laying down a universal rule that all women in public worship ought to cover their hair? One must interpret the principle Paul lays down in 1 Corinthians 11 with what he says here. If a woman's head were always covered, the church would not know if she had her hair braided with gold and pearls. Obviously, Paul is anticipating occasions when a woman's head is not

covered by a veil in corporate worship. I think that what he means in
1 Corinthians 11:1-15 is that if her hair is not a sufficient covering to
proclaim modesty and submission, then she should cover her head (1
Corinthians 11:15).

Although Paul begins by addressing the external aspects of appropriate deportment, he continues by discussing issues of the heart: "but
rather by means of good works, as is proper for women making a
claim to godliness" (v. 10). He makes a contrast. Although outward
dress is important, the internal adornment of godliness is more important. Paul reminds them that there is a manner of life that is appropriate for the woman professing godliness. The phrase "making a
claim" means "profession." A profession of Christ is a profession of
godliness. The word "godliness" means "reverence for God" or "piety." All who are communicant members of the church are to have a
profession of godliness.

This piety expresses itself in a gentle and quiet spirit (1 Peter 3:4).
Moreover, they "are to be reverent in their behavior, not malicious
gossips, nor enslaved to much wine, teaching what is good, so that
they may encourage the young women to love their husbands, to
love their children, to be sensible, pure, workers at home, kind, being
subject to their own husbands" (Titus 2:3-5; 2 Timothy 1:5; 3:15).

Furthermore, this piety expresses itself in the ministry of good works.
Dorcas is a good example of what Paul intends. Her good works are
described in terms of ministry to the needs of others: "this woman
was abounding with deeds of kindness and charity, which she contin-
ually did (Acts 9:36, cf. 39).

Please note that in these passages there is an emphasis on what I call
domestic piety: a woman's godliness is displayed in her domestic responsibilities. We recognize that in God's wisdom a few women do
not marry, but Paul deals with the general pattern. A woman who
does not marry should still abound in the good works detailed by
Paul and Luke.

From these injunctions, we may also determine a woman's role in the
church; it is basically the same as her role in the home. She contrib-

utes to the beauty of the congregation by demonstrating gentleness, compassion, and sympathy. She is to keep the church attractive, as she keeps her home. She is to teach children and other women. She is to serve tables and minister to the widows, the poor, and the destitute. A woman who devotes herself to these things would not have time to involve herself in teaching men or exercising authority.

Her Behavior in Public Worship (v. 11)

Paul goes on to discuss her behavior in the public assembly in verse 11: "A woman must quietly receive instruction with entire submissiveness." Paul repeats briefly what he said in greater detail in 1 Corinthians 14:34-35: "The women are to keep silent in the churches; for they are not permitted to speak, but are to subject themselves, just as the Law also says. If they desire to learn anything, let them ask their own husbands at home; for it is improper for a woman to speak in church."

We note that Paul has in mind chiefly the public assembly, because he calls her to the general role of submission to the leadership of the church. In Ephesians 5:22, he commands women to be in submission to their husbands, but here in 1 Corinthians, it is to the men who lead in worship and, by implication, who rule in the church. With these commandments, the apostle gives further instruction for ordering the life of the congregation, namely, those who bear authority in the church are to be men. The injunction to women does not rule out the fact that the Bible directs all members to be in submission to the officers (1 Thessalonians 5:12, 13; Hebrews 13:17), but the submission of women is to manifest itself in silence. As we see in 1 Corinthians 14:34, 35, she is not to speak, except corporately along with the rest of the congregation, nor may she attempt to get around this injunction by using a question to get across her view or to instruct. If she has a genuine question, she is to ask her husband. If she is not married, she should ask her elder.

Therefore, she is not to engage in public speaking. Apart from those acts of worship that are done corporately (unison reading, common prayer, congregational singing, etc.), she is to remain silent. Therefore, women are not to read Scripture or lead in prayer in the public worship of the church.

HER ROLE IN THE RULING/TEACHING OF THE CHURCH

The Prohibition (v. 12)

In verse 12, the apostle expands his teaching on the role of women in the church: "But I do not allow a woman to teach or exercise authority over a man, but to remain quiet." Some interpret this prohibition as one commandment — "I do not allow a woman to teach authoritatively" — to avoid the prohibition against exercising authority or to say that she may teach in the public assembly as long as it is under the authority of the officer bearers and not in her own authority. Such interpretations are grammatically indefensible. The text clearly makes the term "man" the object of both prohibitions.

Hence, the first prohibition is "I do not allow a woman to teach [a man]." In the context, he is talking about the public assembly. She is not to exercise any public teaching role in public worship. "[She is] to remain quiet."

How do we reconcile this with 1 Corinthians 11:5 which states: "But every woman who has her head uncovered while praying or prophesying, disgraces her head, for she is one and the same as the woman whose head is shaved"? Let us note first that if her prophecy were delivered in the public assembly (there is no record of such in the New Testament), she was not teaching or exercising authority. She was a mouthpiece for the Lord. Second, in the Pastoral Epistles, the Apostle Paul is laying down the instruction for the church in the era between the time of the Apostles and the return of Christ. Paul, assuming the cessation of the special revelatory gift of prophecy, commands women to be silent.

Although he lays down this commandment in the context of public worship, he is, by implication, talking about any formal teaching of men. In other words, in any gathering of the church for instruction, she is not to teach men. The term "teach" is broader in scope than the term "preach." All preaching must teach, but not all teaching is preaching. Thus, whether in a Sunday School class or a Bible study in which men are present, she is not to teach. As noted earlier, she may teach other women and children. But she is not formally to teach men.

I use the word formally because of the example of Priscilla and Aquila in Acts 18:26, "But when Priscilla and Aquila heard him [Apollos], they took him aside and explained to him the way of God more accurately." In the fellowship of the body of Christ, men and women learn from one another. In the home, husbands and wives may instruct informally. But publicly, women are to be silent. This prohibition includes Bible conferences and seminars as well.

As noted above, Paul gives a second prohibition: not to exercise authority over men. This prohibition indicates that acts that form part of the leading of worship are authoritative and, hence, must be performed by those to whom Christ has given this authority. This commandment, however, goes beyond the formal, structured times of public worship and encompasses the broader life of the church. The Authorized Version (King James) translates the word "to usurp authority," but there is no idea of usurpation in this word at all. It means "to exercise" or "to have authority." Obviously, if she takes authority not given to her, she is usurping it. Women are not to exercise rule or authority in the church of the Lord Jesus Christ. Christ has ordained men to be elders and deacons.

The Basis (vv. 13, 14)

Some respond to this prohibition by saying that Paul is dealing with a cultural phenomenon of his day or a situation peculiar to the Ephesian congregation. He anticipates this type of objection by demonstrating clearly that his commandment is rooted in the creation account: "For it was Adam who was first created, and then Eve. And it was not Adam who was deceived, but the woman being deceived, fell into transgression."

In 1 Corinthians 14:34 he grounds his instruction in the law, "just as the Law also says." In 1 Timothy, he derives two arguments from the law. By the term "law," he is referring to the Genesis account of creation and the fall.

The first argument is woman's place in creation; she was created second: "For it was Adam who was first created, and then Eve." He refers to the creation of Adam and Eve in Genesis 2:7, 18-25. Paul's language reflects the creation account. The word translated "created" is literally "formed." The Greek translation (the Septuagint) of Genesis 2:7 uses this word: "Then the LORD God formed man of dust from the ground." In other words, God created man first. Afterwards, he "fashioned," literally built, Eve out of the body of Adam (Genesis 2:22). Paul infers from the order of creation the headship of husbands and male leadership in the church. He spells this principle out in greater detail in I Corinthians 11:8-9, "For man does not originate from woman, but woman from man; for indeed man was not created for woman's sake, but woman for the man's sake."

Paul says it was God's intention from the beginning to place women under male headship. In no way is he implying that women are inferior or less valuable than men; they are created equally in the image of God (Genesis 1:27) and they are equal in Christ (Galatians 3:28). But God has ordained this authority structure. It is important to note as well that this order is a pre-fall order and not a post-fall reality. God has ordained male leadership for the well-being of the home and the church.

Paul develops his second argument from the fall, namely, a woman's susceptibility to deception: "And it was not Adam who was deceived, but the woman being deceived, fell into transgression" (v. 14). Please note that Paul is referring to Eve's confession, "The serpent deceived me, and I ate" (Genesis 3:13). You see how the argument runs: she removed herself from her husband's authority and Satan deceived her.

Paul is saying that she is not to teach men or exercise authority because of her susceptibility to deception. Such teaching is not popular today, but we are ignoring an important biblical principle if we neglect to follow Paul on this point. A woman's strength lies in her gentleness, compassion, and intuition. The family and the church need these things very much. But in her strengths, lie her vulnerability. God has not made her to exercise the kind of hard, judgmental discernment that is necessary in theological and Scriptural issues. By nature, a woman will more likely fall prey to the subtleties of mental and theological error.

It seems that the church should give broader application to Paul's argument than just to the matter of a woman's not teaching men or exercising authority. If she is more susceptible to deception, then, when she teaches other women and children in the church, she should use materials approved by the elders. What about women writing books or curriculum materials for use in the church? A book has the function of being a private teacher. Reading a book is like having a conversation; the reader may have dialogue with the material being read, and either accept or reject it. When the church uses material written by a woman, it needs to be approved by the elders.

HER ROLE IN THE LIFE OF THE CONGREGATION (V. 15)

Paul concludes this section by stating the general principle that governs a woman's role in the church: "But women will be preserved [saved] through the bearing of children if they continue in faith and love and sanctity with self-restraint." Up to this point, Paul has been dealing with woman, in the singular, the woman in the church, but now he lays down a general principle for all women.

He continues to use the Genesis account. In Genesis 3:15, when God curses the snake, He says that the seed of the woman shall destroy the serpent (the devil), "And I will put enmity between you and the woman, and between your seed and her seed; He shall bruise you on the head, and you shall bruise him on the heel." God promises to deliver His people from Satan and sin by a miraculously provided Savior. Biologically and biblically, the seed comes from the man, but here He promises that the deliverer will come from a woman. In this promise, we have an intimation of the virgin conception and birth. In Genesis 3:16, God highlights a woman's role in child-bearing: "To the woman He said, 'I will greatly multiply your pain in childbirth, in pain you will bring forth children.'" Although He accentuates ease of conception and pain in birth, because of her sin, He positively promises that she shall bear children. In the children of a righteous woman, God will bring forth His righteous seed. From that seed, He will bring the Savior. He will, however, continue to use her after the coming of the Savior to bring a righteous seed into the church. For this reason, Adam names her "Eve, because she was the mother of all the living" (Genesis 3:20).

And so, her salvation being through the bearing of children is a direct reference to Genesis 3:15, 16. The primary role of women in the kingdom of God is domestic. She shall bear children and rear them to serve God. Regardless of the numbers of people saved from the world, the greatest number of saved men and women shall come through the Christian home, for those whom God saves from the world and brings into the church will establish Christian homes through which God will build up the church (Psalm 128:5, 6). Women contribute to the kingdom by the bearing and rearing of covenant children. What a glorious privilege! It is true that the hand that rocks the cradle rules the world.

We recognize that most women are to be married and to have children. In God's providence there are exceptions, but this is God's norm for women. Those who do not marry or do not have children are as important, and they too will assist the church and the families in covenant formation.

Paul, however, does not divorce a woman's role from her character. He qualifies his statement: "If they continue in faith and love and sanctity with self-restraint." It is faith in Christ Jesus that saves and enables us to love God and our neighbor. The love through which faith expresses itself is the love that is shaped by the law of God. Women who persevere in this faith and love will be holy — that is, they will be growing in sanctification, dying to sin and become more Christ like. Such a woman will govern wisely. The word translated "self-restraint" is the term used in verse 9 "discreetly." By concluding with this word, Paul brings the discussion back to modesty and chastity. She will be profitable as she remains in submission, accepting her role in the life of the congregation.

Dr. Joseph A. Pipa, Jr. is President of Greenville Presbyterian Theological Seminary, and Professor of Historical & Systematic Theology. This chapter was taken from his "Leading in Worship," originally posted on www.josephpipa.com.

OTHER TITLES PUBLISHED BY THE PRESBYTERIAN PRESS

Reformed Spirituality: Communing with our Glorious God

The Covenant: Gods Voluntary Condescension

Written for our Instruction: The Sufficiency of Scripture for All of Life

A Christian Worldview: Essays from a Reformed Perspective

Sanctification: Growing in Grace

Interpreting & Teaching the Word of Hope: Essays in Honor of Jack Brown Scott on His Seventy-Seventh Birthday

Confessing Our Hope: Essays Celebrating the Life and Ministry of Morton H. Smith

Notes on Ecclesiology by Thomas E. Peck

Essays on the Church of God by John Mitchell Mason

Family Religion by Rev. B.M. Smith

The Presbyterian Standards by Francis R. Beattie

The Subscription Debate by Morton H. Smith

How is the Gold Become Dim by Morton H. Smith

Systematic Theology by Morton H. Smith

J.B. Shearer's Bible Studies